The Years Were Good

THE YEARS
WERE GOOD

by Louis B. Seltzer

INTRODUCTION BY BRUCE CATTON

THE WORLD PUBLISHING COMPANY

Cleveland and New York

Library of Congress catalog card number: 56–10431

FIRST EDITION

INTRODUCTION

You don't always know, at the moment, when you are brushing elbows with somebody special. I first saw Louis B. Seltzer one summer day, thirty-five years ago or thereabouts, when as a very junior reporter I was covering the Cuyahoga County Court House for The Cleveland News. Into the reporters' room, one dull afternoon, there wandered a slight, sandy-haired, baby-faced young man who more or less looked as if he had lost his way and would not quite know what to do after he found it; he disclosed that he was Louie Seltzer and that he worked for The Cleveland Press, and he picked up a telephone and mumbled something into it. Then he sauntered away, and the afternoon game of black-jack was resumed. It did not seem as if anybody in particular had appeared.

5

About two days later I began to see the light, when I learned that this innocent had beaten the daylights out of me on a story of some interest to my City Editor; but it was quite a few years before I realized that I had then met one of the most remarkable men whom the rather unusual city of Cleveland has produced in this century. Nobody knew it at the time, but he was then beginning an extremely useful career in the course of which he would finally emerge as Mr. Cleveland. This career has had an impact which has often driven strong men to the use of very strong language, but its ultimate effect has been very good indeed. It would be possible to argue that he is today the best and most effective newspaper editor in America.

Cleveland is not entirely like other American cities. It is immense, industrious, wealthy, full of energy and also of contradictions, a singular blend of satisfied conservatism and restless liberalism. It is at all times ready to boast of its baseball team and of its symphony orchestra, of the pious solidity of its bankers and of its maverick tradition in politics; it seems to sprawl across half of northern Ohio, and strangers occasionally find it hard to say just what the city is all about. A friend of mine who recently moved there from the East says he is not convinced that there really is any such city. There is, he admits, a vast place where raw materials are turned into finished goods, and where the finished goods in turn are changed into money—but a city? He is not sure.

Seltzer himself would have little patience with such an attitude. If the city itself is a slightly uneasy blend of the Western Reserve and the children of all of middle

Europe, a town which narrowly missed becoming Detroit and which has been half regretful and half elated
over that miss ever since, it is primarily a lot of people
—upwards of a million of them. It is the distillation of
all of their dreams and needs, their victories and de-
feats, their times of confusion and their moments of
insight. Understanding the city itself is not so hard if
you begin by understanding people; if the whole of the
city is sometimes greater than the sum of its parts, the
same is true of every human individual.

Seltzer starts with the people, and he never lets himself get very far away from them. Somewhere in this
account of his life he undertakes to define the job of
editing a newspaper. Properly speaking, he says, editing
is "the endless, sometimes thankless job of keeping at
the primary business of living with, understanding, and
being sympathetic toward all people."

This job he is well qualified to perform. No door-to-
door political campaigner ever did a more thorough,
consistent job of keeping in touch with his constituents
than this editor has done. When the Scripps-Howard
organization turned The Cleveland Press over to Seltzer, nearly thirty years ago, he reflected on the responsibility that had come to him and concluded that it was
above everything else important for him to get into the
job "something of the human qualities that the people
whom I had visited wanted so much."

To that credo he has been consistently faithful, and
The Press today is his elongated shadow. Like its Editor, the paper is frequently exasperating, and sometimes it is mistaken, but it is never in the least stuffy. If

7

The Press speaks with many voices and at times falls into error and self-contradiction, it never strikes the note of father-knows-best; for better or for worse—and net it is very much for the better—it stays close to the people. This is a boast which not too many metropolitan newspapers are able to make.

The era of personal journalism in the United States is supposed to be dead, and one of the things chiefly responsible for its death is alleged to be the newspaper chain. The career of Louis Seltzer indicates that personal journalism is as lively as it ever was—and, be it noted, he is Editor of a chain newspaper. All that is needed, apparently, is a personality of force and fresh intelligence.

Such a personality exists here. The personality is one of the things that have helped to give Cleveland its own distinctive character; it is also one of the things of which Cleveland (and American journalism in general) has most right to be proud.

BRUCE CATTON

June 14, 1956

ILLUSTRATIONS

The Years Were Good

PREFACE

I LIVE for tomorrow. I can scarcely wait until it comes. To be sure, yesterday was interesting. Of course, today is the immediate challenge. But, tomorrow is for the plans, for the dreams, and for the reaching up.

It has been that way ever since as a small boy I began to wonder what life was all about. And if again I were granted the chance of reliving my life, not a solitary thing would be changed—nothing added, nothing subtracted.

It has been, and it is, an exciting, lifting, exhilarating life, both hard and good, dismaying sometimes, oftener otherwise. I have been singularly blessed to work in a profession I love, in my home city which I worship, and at the side of the only girl I have ever known—and whom I adore today even more than when forty years

13

ago, as this book relates, I first looked into her brown eyes.

Struggle is good for the soul. I have had my full share of it. It is shaping, building, strengthening, even when, at times, it seems almost intolerable. I have had no time for worry, and even less for self-pity. Nothing more sharply or more deeply cuts into the ability to meet today and tomorrow—and their problems—than to worry or feel regret.

My heart has always gone out to the children of the rich. I feel for them. Little of my sympathy has been reserved for the children of the poor. I am one of them. I am proud so to be regarded.

The sheltered child who has much is denied the sharp contrasts which give life its true meaning. The appreciation of life comes only from living it—being a part of its struggle, its sacrifice, its tragedy, its self-denial, its heartache, its making nothing to be something—even from feeling hunger, desolation, misery. The child psychologist may squirm at this. Nevertheless I believe that a good measure of these experiences is more often good than bad for a child. For these are inescapably the ingredients of character, of personality, of compassion, of sympathy, of understanding—the contrasts without which a child's growth is not complete, or full, or with perspective.

I like living, for example, in the north country of changing seasons. I like the chilling cold of winter and the almost intolerable heat of summer—the swift transition from color to the attractive grays and blacks of fall, and winter's imminence—the contrasts which make appreciation deep and vivid. I would not wish the monotony of a steady, unchanging climate.

Because as a boy I wore patches on the seat of my britches and shoes whose soles were stuffed with cardboard as I walked through winter's snow, I appreciate good clothes the more as a man. Because as a boy I ate stale bread larded and salted to give it a flavor it did not have, I appreciate food the more.

My heart beats with those who today are suffering those deprivations, yet I do not feel truly sorry for them—except when health is actually endangered and souls are permanently damaged.

Within those limits deprivation will be good for them. They will be better men and women for it. When these things are experienced throughout the making years—the shaping and testing years—the years that children of moderate and poor circumstances will know best and remember longest—they are truly the good years.

It is to these years—to those who have seen them—to those who all over America and the world are now seeing them and will be lifted and strengthened by them—that this book, *The Years Were Good,* is put between these covers.

—L. B. S.

Chapter 1

MY FATHER wrote and published well over forty books. Another two hundred of his stories were printed in magazines. Many of them were made into Hollywood movies, featuring some of the great stars of the old silent films—Douglas Fairbanks, Sr., William S. Hart, Anna Q. Nilsson, Bert Lytell, Harry Carey, Tom Mix, and others.

But when I was seven years old, not a line of his writing had ever been bought by anyone.

It was not because he didn't try. I have never seen anyone who tried as hard as my father, or anyone who was set back so often, only to come back fighting, the way he did. To write he went without food, without sleep, without everything.

Manuscript after manuscript would go out, each

neatly wrapped by my mother. In each package there would be enough postage to return it to our address, and the stamps represented the cost of a meal for our family.

And time after time they came back. Enough rejection slips arrived at our house to paper the little parlor, and always they said the same thing:

"We have read your very interesting manuscript but find it unsuitable for our purpose."

It got so that by simply sighting the postman a half block away we all knew what he'd hand us.

Then one day there was a change in the familiar routine. I will never forget that day.

It started out just like any other. Mother got up early—very early—as she always did on washdays, especially in midsummer. My father called to her in protest.

"Ella, can't you rest a while longer? It isn't even five yet."

"Charlie, be quiet," she whispered. "You'll wake up the children. I'll be all right. I don't want to wait until the heat gets unbearable."

Their voices came through the thin walls of our little, three-room frame house and awakened me. I came to the door.

"Can I please get up, Mother, too, so's I can finish my kite?"

At first I thought she'd send me back to bed, but she reconsidered, saying, "Yes, I suppose so. But you stay out from under my feet, and don't get this kitchen all messed up with your paste and stuff."

Kite-making was my obsession, and she knew it. One

night not long before Father had grabbed me by my nightshirt as I was climbing over the transom in my sleep to go out and fly a double-decker red-white-and-blue Uncle Sam kite I had just made.

"Before you get started with that kite you can do something for me," Mother said, as I stood in the kitchen hitching up my overalls, and rubbing sleep from my eyes. "Get me a couple of pails of water from outside."

There wasn't much room in the kitchen. In one corner was a potbellied stove which kept the house fairly warm in winter. In the other was a coal range, where my mother heated up all the water for washing and cooked our food. Already she had a big pan of water getting hot on the range.

Her washday equipment was kept outside the kitchen door on a big stoop just big enough for a sack of coal, kindling wood, and a tub. The big wooden tub, bound by iron bands, served two family purposes. It was Mother's washtub. It was also the family bathtub. I stumbled over it as I brought the water in.

"One more thing you can do, Louis," Mother said. "You can cut the soap for me."

This I liked to do. She handed me a huge chunk of mottled homemade soap and a pan. I took her big, nicked butcher knife and sliced off a whole pan full of soap, which she sprinkled liberally over the clothes steaming on the stove. Perspiration was already running in tiny streams over her face, under the small towel wrapped around her head.

Father came into the kitchen, hitching up his galluses.

"Ella, can I do anything to help?"

"Yes," Mother said. "You can keep watch for the postman this morning. That'll be your job. Somehow I have a premonition something is going to happen."

Father started to protest.

"Now, get out, get out," she pretended to scold him, sweeping him aside with the broom she was vigorously applying to the kitchen floor. "I have to get breakfast for your hungry ones."

My kite was finished. Daylight had come, and my younger brothers and sisters were getting up. The sun started to climb above a cloudless horizon, and the heat of a midwestern summer day was settling down upon us. I ran after the tall, black-haired figure walking toward the old well in the center of our small yard. "Daddy," I begged, "would you help me get my kite up?"

Obligingly, Father held the kite in the street. I ran a half block away. At my signal, he let go and I sprinted. The kite slowly went into the air, caught the current, and spiraled swiftly up until all my string had been let out. This time I had made a red-and-green one with white fringe running all around it, and it looked beautiful against the deep blue sky. For a couple of hours I gave no thought to anything else. I sat on the curb, completely lost in contemplation of my triumph, idly wondering, if I had all the string in the world, whether the kite could go to the moon.

I felt a tap on my shoulder. It was the postman, Mr. Saunders.

"Louis, I have something here for your father," he said. "Would you want to take it in?"

Suddenly awakened from my lazy dream, I literally backed away from him. I recalled my mother's feeling that something was going to happen, and a sense of uneasiness began to creep over me.

"You better take it, Mr. Saunders," I said. "I'll have to get my kite down. Mother wants it—she wants it right away, I think."

My excitement grew, and I started to pull in my kite, but it was too slow. I tied the string around a fence picket, and ran as fast as I could to our house the half block down the street. I got there just as Mr. Saunders walked up the stone flagging to our front door.

Mother was waiting for him. She took one look at the envelope he handed her and let out a shriek that could be heard all over the neighborhood.

"Charlie, Charlie—children, children, children, come here, quick—come here quick everybody!" she shouted.

Everybody came tumbling into the small parlor where Mother stood, her eyes wide in excitement, her hands shaking so hard she almost dropped the envelope.

Father came running into the house.

"Charlie, look—look at this!"

My father looked at the envelope. He looked at Mother. He looked at us. I wondered for an instant if he was going to cry.

"Open it, Charlie, for goodness sake, open it—the suspense is terrible," Mother said, half crying, half laughing.

"What does it say?" we all cried, crowding around as Father's nervous fingers tore at the envelope.

"Here, Ella," he said finally. "You open it. I can't. My hand is too shaky."

Mother took the envelope, and with one strong rip tore it open. A slip of paper fell out.

"A check, Charlie—a check," Mother shouted. She pushed the letter back into Father's hands, but didn't wait for him to read it. The tension built up during years of sacrifice, based on her faith and confidence in her husband's writing, suddenly gave way. She let out a mighty Indian war whoop and started circling around the table, waving the check over her head. We fell into line behind her and followed, one by one—all of us shouting, dancing, waving our arms, almost bringing the house down with our noise and stomping.

At first Father stood watching us, looking stunned and bewildered. Then a broad smile lit up his face, and, bending over low like an Indian chief joining the war dance, he let out a tremendous whoop, and the shouting, dancing, noise, and stomping against the floor boards got louder than ever.

Mother and Father embraced each other, the tears openly streaming down their faces, while we made a circle around them, still shouting and dancing. It took a long time for the excitement to subside.

When it did at last, Father read aloud the short letter that Mr. Saunders had left at our house. I can still remember it word for word:

> Your short story, "Mary Jane's Diversion" is accepted by us for publication. It is an interesting story and well

written. We are herewith inclosing a check for $25, in payment thereof. We would be happy to have you submit others of your manuscripts.

The letter was from *Short Story* magazine. We were absolutely quiet while he read, and when he finished, only Mother's subdued sobbing could be heard. Father put his arm around her, and said, "Ella, this is the beginning. Now I feel that I can do it."

Mother looked at him smiling through her tears. "Charlie, we will never cash that check," she said. "I am going to get Mr. Leroux to frame it, and we'll keep it—keep it always."

Chapter 2

MR. BELZ was beaming happily. He appeared to be expecting us, for the bell had scarcely started to tinkle when he opened the door leading into his neat white butcher shop.

"So I read in the paper Poppa has already sold a story, yes?" he said. His round, red face was creased with many pleasurable wrinkles.

He wiped his hands energetically on what at an earlier hour of the day had been an immaculately white apron; it was now flecked with the blood of his wares.

"Maybe now things will be different, yes, Mrs. Seltzer?" he suggested, half questioningly. "What will it be today, now? We have—"

But Mother interrupted him. "Mr. Belz, I must tell you something first. We haven't paid our bill yet and I'm afraid we can't."

I looked up at Mother. Her face had a strained expression, and her hands twisted anxiously around her market bag.

"It's true Charlie sold a story," she said, "but selling one story after all these years, wonderful as it is, is not much help. We don't know yet what will happen. We hope it will be all right, but we can't tell. I know Charlie will try—"

Mr. Belz leaned his fat arms on the counter, a deep frown on his usually friendly face.

Even under normal circumstances he dominated his small shop. His own personal width occupied fully a third of the space behind his counter. He had always seemed as wide as he was high. Now he appeared gigantic.

Mother's growing nervousness affected me. I suddenly took an interest in her market bag because it brought me closer and more protectively near her.

For a long moment Mr. Belz was silent. He seemed to be thinking his way through a problem, weighing it as carefully as if it were on the scales at his elbow. Finally he lifted his eyes, and looked squarely at Mother. There was a funny little smile on his lips.

"Mrs. Seltzer, I am surprised by you," he said. "Have I ever asked you for money, yet? Why should I be doing so now, please? Do I not know what you have been doing—do I not know about the brown paper, the way you've been working to help Charlie? Do I not know these things—was I born yesterday? I am ashamed you should bring it up. And now, Mrs. Seltzer, what are we going to have today, yes?"

He reached over the counter and put his big, pudgy hand on Mother's rather gently. "And I suppose we will also want some more brown paper, will we not?" he asked.

"Yes, yes, Mr. Belz," Mother said, "and thank you so much. We'll pay our bill one of these days, I promise you—you can be sure of that."

Mother finished her purchases and we were on our way out when Mr. Belz called to me.

"Louis," he said softly, "look!"

In his hands he held a nice large slice of summer sausage.

"Thank you, Mr. Belz," I said, the words and the sausage meeting one another.

"Louis," the butcher said, "be a good boy, and help your Momma—she needs it."

When we got home Father was waiting for us. He had written three pages of a new story and then run out of paper. Mother put her market bag down, fished out the brown butcher paper Mr. Belz had given her, and whacked off a sheet.

Having thus satisfied Father's immediate need, she went rather deliberately about the job of converting the big roll of paper into makeshift manuscript sheets for his stories. For this she had contrived a complicated but, for her purpose, effective procedure. I watched as she folded the paper like an accordion until she had a large pile in front of her. Then she went to the kitchen drawer and got out her breadboard. It had been in the family for three generations and was chipped and white with continual use and scrubbing. Mother had added marks of her own to it, not only on top, but on the underside, where she had grooved a deep and perfect rectangle the exact size of the expensive paper they could not afford to buy at Alderson's Stationery Store up on West Twenty-fifth Street.

Carefully, she placed the pile of paper on the bread-board over the square she had grooved in it, and weighted it down with a paving brick she kept in a corner near the door, which otherwise served as a door-stop.

After she made sure the stack of paper was in exact position, she started the sharp tip of the knife around the groove, feeling her way with the knife's edge. It looked hard to do, but to Mother, after long practice, the job was simple. In a surprisingly quick time she lifted off the brick and picked up a neat stack of about twenty sheets.

Patiently she repeated the process until, at the end of a half hour, she had prepared approximately 250 sheets—a supply that might, with normal writing, last Father perhaps a week or ten days.

After neatly arranging the whole batch, Mother placed it in a box at Father's elbow on the table, stopping long enough to kiss him lightly on the forehead as she did so. Father looked up—smiled appreciatively—and then went on with his work.

Mother shoved us out of the kitchen. It was a rule of the house—established by Mother and rigidly en-forced by her—that when Father wrote there was to be absolute quiet. When he chose to write in the daytime, our cruising range around the house was restricted a great deal. For one thing we were deprived of access to the water pail that stood near the little table he used for a desk. Mother's cupboard, almost at Father's writing arm, also was off limits. We solved this problem by stocking up our provisions in a small wooden bucket with a galvanized iron cover, that was placed just outside the kitchen door. Into it we put everything we would need while Father wrote—cookies, bread, candy, kite string, Indian feathers, pocketknives for mumblety-peg, a broken cup to scoop up water from the well bucket near the house, and a host of other miscellaneous articles that were sure to come in handy for a robust family of five children, bent on play and a normal quota of juvenile mischief.

Fortunately for us Father didn't write very often during the day. His "inspirations," as he called them, came much more frequently at night. Every night he arranged the kitchen table in a corner a short distance from the potbellied stove, placed the lamp on it, and pulled up the straight-backed chair with the cane seat which had almost sprung apart. Any night I expected to hear a thud and see my father sprawled on the floor. I kept wondering, if Father actually did fall through the chair, how, with his big bulk, he would get himself out of it.

Mother's faith in Father was so great that we looked upon him with awe and respect, because she did. She tried in every way to protect him from the cares and troubles which came from not having enough of anything to provide for a family. Even at a very early age we children sensed the crisis in which we lived. We knew what Father was trying to do, and what Mother was doing to help him accomplish it.

Father had had very little education. He did not finish the second grade in public school in Columbus, Ohio, where his family had lived before they moved to Cleveland.

Our grandfather used to tell us, much to Mother's chagrin, that when Father was a small boy he ran away from home and joined the Sells-Floto circus as a water boy for the elephants. Any romantic detail about this exploit that was inadvertently overlooked by Grandpa was supplied by Father himself. Of all the varied jobs he had after he slipped away from grade school, never to return—and to acquire such remarkable education as he put together for himself by his own experience, his extraordinary gifts for observation, concentration, and imagination—the one which obviously intrigued him most of all was that of water boy for Sells-Floto circus. He talked about it often.

This was only one of many things Father did during the fifteen years before he came to Cleveland and "settled down." He was successively steeplejack's assistant, himself climbing to the top of some of the higher church steeples; floorwalker in a five-and-ten-cent store; railroad brakeman and handy man; and cowpuncher in New Mexico. For several years he was an itinerant typesetter and a writer for small-town newspapers, working in several places where his favorite author, Mark Twain, had labored; and, like Mark Twain, he was an intense lover of the land along the Mississippi River.

One day in October, when Mother had brought in a new supply of butcher's brown paper, Father wrote steadily for hours. He took out very little time for dinner. Restlessly he walked up and down outside for a breath of fresh air, while we all pitched in to clear the table and wash the dishes as quickly as possible. Then, as twilight came, he eagerly took up his place once more at his "desk."

Everybody went to bed—except Father and myself.

There were only two sounds in the small kitchen as the evening wore on, and midnight was imminent. One was the cracking of coal behind the isinglass "window" of the potbellied stove before which I lay reading. The other was the scratch of Father's pen, as he sat bent over the small table in the flickering light from the kerosene lamp.

I was lost to everything except the engrossing story of the prince who vainly tried to climb the glass mountain to rescue the princess. The weird shadows fashioned so grotesquely by the dancing flames of the stove heightened the strange world to which Grimm's fairy tale had transported me.

Both Father and I were so completely intent upon our respective interests that neither of us heard Mother step softly into the kitchen. Not until I felt the sharp pinch of her fingers on my left ear did I know she was near-by.

"I have called you for the last time, Louis—and now off to bed you march, young man—this instant!"

She emphasized her order with a sharp tweak on my

ear and a propulsion at the rear end which sent me scrambling off-balance toward the bedroom.

On my way I heard her say, turning her attention to Father, "You two—always you two. Louis always reading, reading, reading. He's going to ruin his eyes. Why can't you help me with him, Charlie—he's as much your responsibility as mine. But you're just as bad as he is. Off to bed now—both of you!"

My father sat stubbornly at his "desk," mumbling, "Just a little while, Ella."

Mother stood uncertainly at his side while I watched from the bedroom doorway, hoping also to be reprieved. Then she turned her wrath and her worry in my direction. "I thought I told you to get to bed, young man. Now get!"

With one flying leap I jumped into bed, almost pushing my brother Bob, sound asleep, out and onto the floor. He managed to save himself by grabbing a bedpost.

I didn't go off to sleep immediately. For a long time I lay in bed listening to the steady scratching of Father's pen and speculating on whether the prince finally made it up the mountain. The suspense was intolerable, but I knew what disaster would befall me if again I slipped out into the kitchen to retrieve my book and find out. After a long time, and in half sleep, I heard Mother's voice, raised this time to an anxious pitch.

"Charlie, stop now? It must be three o'clock. You'll just get another of those terrible headaches."

The scratching of the pen stopped, but only for a moment.

"Ella," my father said, "I'll be all right. I'm almost finished with this now."

Finally, I fell asleep. I don't know how long I slept, but I was awakened by Mother shaking me roughly.

"Louis, Louis—wake up. Run for Dr. Medlin, quick! It's Daddy—something's wrong—something's awful wrong!"

The excited words got me onto my feet in a second. Already she had thrown off the quilt and had my pants and shirt and shoes in her hands ready for me to put on.

"Oh, hurry, Louis—hurry," she kept repeating over and over again.

I got into my clothes faster than ever before, and dashed through the kitchen toward the door. On the way I was shocked to see Father lying on the kitchen floor, right beside the cane-seated chair at his little desk. Even without stopping I noticed that his face was white, that he didn't move. Mother was wiping his forehead with a cold towel as I raced out.

It was dark, and cold. On other nights when I went on an errand for Mother every corner held a ghost or a frightful creature lurking to jump out at me; every post and pole concealed some horrible giant or weird animal. These were all forgotten. Only one thing mattered. Father was sick, desperately sick, and it was my job to get Dr. Medlin just as fast as my legs would carry me.

From our house to Dr. Wendell Medlin's was about

a half mile. I don't know how long it took me that early morning to make it. A stitch in my side made breathing hard, but I plunged on at breakneck speed, sometimes tripping, almost stumbling and falling several times as broken pavement or rocks got in my way. But I kept blindly on—pushing my legs, gasping for breath. All the time I kept thinking, "If I don't get there in time, if I don't get there in time, something terrible might happen to Father."

At last, exhausted and out of breath, I reached Dr. Medlin's house, threw open the gate and ran up the front walk to the steps. I pounded the heavy iron knocker against the door. It sounded loud in the stillness of the early morning.

The doctor didn't come—I kept pounding.

A flickering light came on at last, and an irritable voice sounded: "I'm coming—I'm coming. Stop that infernal racket."

And Dr. Medlin, a large, heavily built man, appeared in the doorway. He was wearing a long, flowing nightshirt with a startling pattern on it which under other circumstances would have made me laugh. He was still rubbing the sleep out of his eyes with his free hand, holding the flickering candle in the other.

"Who in tarnation is it?" he asked, looking at a level above my head, evidently expecting to see an adult. He looked down and saw me. "Why, Louis, it's you! What are you doing here at this hour? What's wrong, Son?"

My breath was coming back though my chest still ached.

"It's Daddy, Doctor—it's Daddy. Mother says for you to come right away, please! Hurry, he's lying on the kitchen floor. Something awful has happened."

Without a word, Dr. Medlin turned around, and leaving the door open, made for his bedroom.

"Louis, you wait out by the barn for me, I'll be there right away," he called over his shoulder.

Obediently I went to the barn at the rear of the rambling old house. Now some of the ghosts and evil creatures of the night began to reappear, but only the sight of my father lying so quiet and white-faced on the kitchen floor would stay long in my mind. I did not even feel the cold of the October dawn, though frost was gleaming under the bright moon and stars, on the roofs and fences and even on the grass.

Dr. Medlin's barn was quite a way back from his house. I opened the door. Against wide cracks at the far end of the stable I could see the silhouette of his dapple-gray horse, who had what seemed to me the crazy name of Rameses. The horse chomped at the side of his stall and neighed at me. He seemed to know that he would be called upon, as frequently he was, to go out into the night with the doctor.

Dr. Medlin appeared, still buttoning his coat, carrying his black case.

"Get up in that one," he instructed, nodding toward the two-seater carriage.

With quick, sure movements, he led Rameses from his stable, moved him into his traces, deftly fastened the leather harness, and climbed into the driver's seat.

34

"Now, Louis," he said. "That didn't take long, did it?"

His voice was now gentle and kind. He wrapped me in his big robe, and brought me close to him.

"Giddy-yap, Rameses," he ordered, and the horse moved out of the stable, up the drive, and into the street at a quick pace. Once on the unpaved street, bumping and jolting, Dr. Medlin's carriage careened along at as fast a clip as the horse could make it.

"Your Daddy will be all right," Dr. Medlin said, and then, quite obviously to get my boyish mind off my fright, he pointed to the stars.

"Aren't they bright? They always are just before the dawn. It's always darkest then—and then the sun comes up, and everything's all right. It'll be all right, Louis."

In front of our house Dr. Medlin didn't even bother to tether his horse. He walked hurriedly up the walk, opened the door without knocking, and went straight to the kitchen where Father was still lying on the floor with Mother hovering over him.

"Hello, Ella," the doctor said, shortly. "What's happened here?"

Without waiting for Mother's answer, he opened his black bag, brought out his instruments, and gently rolled Father over on his side.

"I don't know, Doctor," Mother said. "I heard him fall. I came out here, and there was Charlie on the floor—right where he is now. He hasn't opened his eyes since. I don't know—" Her voice was rising in alarm.

"Well, don't be excited, now, we'll find out in a minute," Dr. Medlin said.

It seemed an eternity to me before Father opened his eyes, looked bewilderedly around the kitchen, first at Dr. Medlin and then at Mother and then at me. He lay there without saying a word for a little while, and then asked, "What happened?"

Mother rushed over to Father and took him in her arms.

"Now, Ella, let Charlie lie there for a couple of minutes," the doctor said. As Father lay quiet, now with a pillow under his head, he quietly told Mother, "Charlie has been working too hard. He's got to stop writing for a while—for maybe a few weeks, even longer."

Mother explained that she hadn't been able to do anything with Father for months now—"Ever since he sold that first story," she said. "It's write—write—write all the time. He's sent five stories away to magazines in the last month or so. I was afraid something would happen."

Again her voice betrayed her anxiety, and the doctor put his hand on her shoulder, saying, "Well, first let's get him to bed."

Together they helped Father, still bewildered by it all, to bed.

That was the year Father really became our hero. And that was the year I grew up, even though I was only eight, for wasn't I the oldest in the family—the one to whom Mother had turned in time of crisis—the one who now got odd jobs around the neighborhood to help? I felt suddenly important, and indispensable to the household.

Many things happened that winter. Perhaps in weather, in hard times, and certainly within our own home, it was the worst of any we ever experienced. Yet, with Mother's grim determination to make everything come out all right, it did.

Three things happened which left their impress upon me for the rest of my life. Father, virtually helpless for a time, took the attitude that his oldest son, in spite of his tender years, was entitled to adult treatment and attention. Also, that winter I took my place in the household as a breadwinner. I got up before daybreak to carry papers before school. At noon each day I carried Mr. Bell's warm lunch to him from his home up on West Twenty-fifth Street to his barber shop on Fulton Road, a distance of three-quarters of a mile. At night I carried the evening paper—The Cleveland Press— and to wind up the day I worked in the grocery store across the street until it closed.

The third important thing that happened to me that severe winter, when I was just turned eight, was the firm resolve that one day I would be a writer like my hero, my father—and a newspaperman.

Chapter 3

GRANDPA Lucien Bonaparte Seltzer and Uncle Ray came to live at our house that winter soon after Father's serious illness. We were already overcrowded with a family of five small children, but Mother, suddenly faced with the urgent need of bringing income from some source into the house, was confident it could be managed. She saw no reason for Grandpa Lucien Bonaparte—whose initials I have carried through life—and Uncle Ray to pay board and shelter to someone else, and she prevailed upon them to live under our roof.

Living under our roof, literally, is what it turned out they did.

"You two might just as well live here, anyway," Mother told them, in outlining her proposal. "You are here, underfoot, most of the time as it is."

Uncle Ray was quite young at the time, although, because of his powerful physique and remarkable voice, he appeared to us much older than he really was. He was unmarried, and up to this time he had lived with Grandpa Lucien in a single room above a store a couple of miles away from us. Their loneliness was best illustrated by the frequency of their visits to our home.

Ray, like Father, was a carpenter by trade. He had a rich baritone voice, and when on summer evenings we would all sit around the well at the side of our house, Uncle Ray, Father, and Grandpa Lucien Bonaparte lifted their voices in song—and we would sit listening, enthralled.

"I wish you men would stop singing that stuff to these children," Mother would sternly complain to the three men, whose choice of music was not always elegant and whose harmony was somewhat stimulated by periodic trips across Fulton Road to Bill Noss' saloon, for white-capped pails of beer.

"Rushing the growler" was a pleasant part of such summer evenings for us children. As each pail of the amber fluid was exhausted, Grandpa Lucien Bonaparte, the principal mischief-maker of our household, would squint an eye at one of us, and in a confidentially lowered voice—quite obviously so Mother would not hear—would pick out the next courier.

"Louis, it's your turn now. Tell Mr. Noss to fill it up just enough to give it a white froth over the top. And don't spill any of that precious liquid on the way back," he would add in mock severity.

Each time we went through the swinging doors into
Noss' saloon we stopped at the big wicker basket of
pretzels at the near end of the bar, and stuffed our
pockets. The barkeeper seemed to have eyes in the
back of his head, for, without appearing to look our
way, he would say, "All right, Louis, that's just about
enough, Son. We'll have to leave some for the customers
now, won't we?" And then he would ask, "What'll it
be for those tomcat wailers across the street—more of
the same?"

On some evenings the circle by the well was expanded by some of my grandfather's cronies, and the
singing would be suspended in favor of tall tales of
the West and the Civil War and Indian fighting. The
taller the tale the greater the laughter and applause,
and we children, discreetly lying in the shadows outside
of the adult circle, were transported body, spirit, and
soul to the primitive ranges of Texas and New Mexico
and Montana, to Appomattox and Gettysburg, to South
Africa and Asia. As I look back on these tales, I realize
the facts might often have been challenged, but they
had all the color and excitement that these suds-
stimulated spellbinders could contrive from their competitive imaginations.

When more serious matters were discussed, the adult
circle tended to widen in almost the proportion that
the juvenile section of it shrank. When the names of
McKinley and Bryan came up, and silver ratios and
kindred matters were mentioned, we promptly lost all
interest and sought refuge under the street lamp and
on the curb.

But when one adult in particular appeared to take part in these backyard deliberations, stimulated in more than one sense of the word by Mr. Noss' special wares, we battled one another for position in the circle nearest him. This was old Nick Roth, an Indian fighter, a frontiersman, a pal of Buffalo Bill's, a romantic and exciting personality in the neighborhood, and my father's special friend.

He wore a goatee and a sombrero, and on his visits to our house he often brought souvenirs of his adventuresome days in the Old West. His language was as picturesque as his appearance, and we listened to him by the hour as he spun his tales of folks we read about in the paperback novels and magazines current in the early nineteen hundreds. Old Nick brought them vividly, sometimes chillingly, into our lives. We could almost see and hear the war whoops, the rattle of muskets, the shrieks and cries of battle and gun fights in the streets of frontier towns or over the wild and wooly western hills and plains. Mother always seemed to arrive at the most inopportune moment to send us double-quick to bed, but Old Nick was ready with his promise to "continue it the next time."

"How these children ever manage to sleep peacefully after some of the stories you tell them, Nick, I will never know," Mother would complain to the tall, lean, white-haired ex-plainsman.

So it was really not much of a change for Grandpa Lucien and Uncle Ray to move over to our house, and they lost no time in accepting Mother's invitation. She led them into the small kitchen and pointed to a trap door in the ceiling, something that in all the time we had lived in our small house we had never used, or even explored. We had frequently been tempted to find out where that door led, but were always dissuaded by Mother's firm admonition: "Under no circumstances do I want you children—ever—to try to fuss around with that door in the ceiling."

We speculated about it, but never did anything about it, until Grandpa Lucien and Uncle Ray took up lodging at our place.

"Now you two," Mother said to them, "can get busy, since you pretend to be good carpenters, fixing up a place for yourselves up in that attic. I don't know what you'll find up there, but it's my guess you'll find plenty of room if you can work out how to make use of it."

Grandpa Lucien put a ladder under the trap door and climbed up to it, but there was no way to open it.

"Consarn it," he exclaimed, "what a way to do things! The critter who did that ought to have his noodle examined. Such a business. I guess there's only one thing to do, and that's to break right through it, and then fix up a trap door later that really works."

With a hammer and saw Grandpa finally exposed a large hole in the ceiling through which one after the other of us crawled—all except Father, who was still immobilized by the doctor's orders—to survey the one strange and alien place in our house.

Grandpa was first. He bellowed in indignation.

"Why those careless, good-for-nothing, lazy critters," he shouted out, his voice echoing and magnifying in

42

the dark recesses of the attic as if he were far away in a cave. "Just look-a-here, Ray! Why, if either of us ever left around a lot of junk like this they'd put us in jail. Just look at that stuff for a nice fire."

The rest of us climbed up. By the light of a small window at the front of the attic, whose purpose until this moment had been exclusively ornamental because it was never opened, we saw heaps of rubbish, discarded shingles, lumber refuse, plaster, tin, and an incredibly large and varied assortment of materials carelessly left behind by the builders.

"Well," Mother said philosophically, "it will give you men folks something to do while you are figuring out how best to fix up your living quarters here."

It took two days to carry out the accumulated refuse from the attic; most of it, to save Mother's kitchen, was pushed out the attic window onto the small porch roof below—and then dumped onto the ground.

"Now be careful, Ray," warned Grandpa, a frugal man in some respects though prodigal in others—especially when it came to regular and sustained investment in Mr. Noss' establishment across the street. "We can use some of this timber, here. It'll come in handy for a partition or two."

Grandpa and Uncle Ray went faithfully at the job of converting the attic, very small at best, and with the roof sloping abruptly on both sides, into two "bedrooms." The larger of the two they fixed up for themselves. We were curious about the other until it was almost finished, and Mother explained.

"Louis, you are to have a room upstairs with the men

43

folks," she said, obviously, I realized later, trying to soften any unhappiness I might feel at being suddenly removed from my customary place with the rest of the family.

One night we three, Grandpa Lucien, Uncle Ray, and myself, climbed up through the trap door to the attic, using a stepladder built especially for the purpose, and took up our uneasy and not altogether comfortable residence therein. There was no heat except what the chimney gave from the kitchen stove. The ladder was left up all night, and Mother warned, "It's up to you folks to light your own way because I can't have a candle or an oil lamp a-burning in this kitchen all night. Now git, all of you, and you, Grandpa, see to it that this young man gets to sleep at a reasonable time. You know how he is—he'll stay up all night reading. Especially," she added, looking significantly at me, "if he knows I can't see the light from my room."

We might just as well have been sleeping outside that first night. It must have been down around zero, and heavy snow was falling. I bundled myself up with all the bedclothing Mother supplied until only my eyes and nose were free. On the floor beside the little cot they had put in my room—a "room" just big enough for the cot and a kitchen chair beside it for my clothes —I had my kerosene lamp. I had made sure before coming up that it was well filled with kerosene and that the wick was neatly tapered. I had my own ideas of how much reading I would do up in my new room.

"Louis," Grandpa said, about midnight, "your

mother told me to have you put that lamp out. I'm going to be generous with you, young man, but when I tell you to put it out—out it goes, because I'm not going to have you go to sleep on us and burn the whole house down with everybody in it."

Grandpa never had cause to feel that I violated his magnanimous understanding of my feverish devotion to reading. I always obeyed him, and since he, too, liked to stay awake at night reading, the matter was rendered simple all around.

That attic stands out in my memory still, for it was there that I got the best part of my education. One late afternoon, when I came in from delivering my Press route, I overheard Father talking from his bed to my grandfather, and thus I learned quite by accident that he was contriving to guide my reading habits. "I want that boy to read good books," Father was saying, "just like I read. There's a library card around here somewhere, and I want you to go up there and get Louis the books on this list. When he's finished with them I'll jot down the titles of some more."

Shrewdly he chose the most exciting of the books written by the great writers of America and the Old World. It was evident that his devotion to Rudyard Kipling and Charles Dickens was unbounded, because virtually everything they ever wrote appeared on the list he supplied Grandpa Lucien for library borrowing. The first books that appeared on the chair in my room were Mark Twain's, which I thought most natural, in view of Father's great admiration for him.

Somehow the fact that I had overheard Father's plot, instead of arousing my resentment, deepened my interest in the things he wanted me to read.

"How did you find this one?" Grandpa would ask me, with an innocent smile on his face, feigning his part in the plot rather well.

"It's wonderful, Grandpa," I would say. "Have you ever read it?"

"Well, no, can't say as I have," he would reply. "But I know somebody who has." I knew without his telling me who that "somebody" was. It was Father.

"Better ask him," Grandpa said. "He'll tell you how he liked it, and maybe he'll tell you something about it you didn't notice. Why don't you try him?"

That was the second step in Father's plot, and I saw through it only because I had discovered the first. Thus he introduced me to the wonderful host of books which he had read during his life, together with others that now, in his enforced quiet, he was able to read; and he also taught me how to read them, how to get the most out of them.

"Books, Son," he said, "are the most wonderful things in the world. They are the wisdom of all the ages. From them you can get everything you need, provided you read them intelligently and carefully.

"Read the books, Son, with two things in mind—how they are written, and why they are written. Each person who writes a book has something in mind. Some purpose is behind it.

"There are good books and bad books. There are so many good books it's a shame to waste any time reading the bad ones. After you read enough books you can pick one from the other by yourself."

I looked up at him, as he said these last words, for without intending to he had given himself away to me. Realizing it, he looked quickly at me, and saw the knowledge in my eyes.

"Well, Son, what do you think? Have I been a poor chooser?"

"No, they've been wonderful," I told him quickly, and eagerly. "You know which one I am reading now?"

"No," Father said, "but I think I can guess."

"I'll give you three guesses," I said, thinking I might trip him up.

"Well, I'll tell you, Louis," he said, "you are giving it away by giving me three guesses—I'd guess all three of them the same way, *The Three Musketeers.*"

Father said a lot of things that day that I remember —about his own way of educating himself, and about the discipline of constant and wise reading. My childish admiration for him increased, even though I could not at the time completely take in the tremendous accomplishment of this almost totally uneducated man over the beauty of thoughts and words.

One day when I climbed up to my attic room after school there were three very large books on the chair. I opened one of them, a large Bible filled with full-page illustrations. Pinned to the first page was a note from Father.

Son, in this little game you and I are having of reading good books I want you to know something that is really important. These books that I have asked Mother to put on the chair in your room are the most important of all ever written. Together they are the Bible.

In the Bible is all of the goodness, and wisdom, and inspiration any of us ever need in life. You have been reading some good books. I think you have learned to appreciate them instead of the trash in the cheap books they're printing nowadays.

I have read the Bible many times. I can't remember really how many. It must be at least a dozen times. I first read it when I was your age. Grandpa did for me what I am trying to do for you. He gave me a Bible and in reading it I found, as I am sure you will, that it is the best book of all.

It may seem hard to read at first. There are things in it you won't understand, and if you have any questions about it I want you to ask me. I am going to leave the Bible up in your room now for a long time. I hope you will read it many times, as I did, and as many other good people have. It gets better each time you read it again. It is filled with wonderful stories. Love, Dad.

This was the first writing he had done, so far as I knew, since he became sick—and it was on his own writing paper, the brown paper Mother brought home from the butcher's and cut especially for him.

Mother's formal schooling was even less than Father's, but, like Father, she had read the Bible over and over. She knew it so well that she could quote exact passages from it, and give the chapter and verse without fail. "Without God in our hearts," she often said, "we are nothing." From the time we were able to talk, she taught us to kneel beside our beds and send up our prayers.

Father was more philosophical about us than she was. When we had been punished, and remorse seized him

for using the hard palm of his hand on a tender spot—
and sometimes his razor strop, if the offense seemed
serious enough to warrant that aggravated treatment—
his standard remark was: "If they just manage to keep
out of jail, I'll be satisfied."

This was always said with a twinkle in his eyes and
a knowing smile on his lips, but Mother could never
take it as a joke.

"Charlie, how can you stand there and even think
such a thing, let alone say it?" she would say, her eyes
blazing with indignation.

The effect was only to bring a wider smile and a mer-
rier twinkle into Father's mischievous eyes. We knew
exactly what he meant—and instinctively caught the
sober message he conveyed in his presumably light-
hearted words.

Perhaps I didn't read the Bible quite as often as my
parents did, but that winter and spring I read it often,
and later in life I managed to read it through at least
three times. I found it to be everything Father said it
was, the best book ever written.

Sooner than either he or I ever dreamed, my school
days were to end, and my ability thereafter was to de-
pend altogether on how much and what I read—and
most important, how wisely I read.

Chapter 4

WHEN I WAS just going on thirteen, and in the seventh grade at Denison School, I reached a decision. I made up my mind to leave school and get a job.

I sat eating my breakfast, watching the worried expression on Mother's face as she moved about the kitchen. Even the breakfast this morning was a reason for me to go to work. It consisted of corn meal mush and hard bread. I knew about the unpaid bill at Friedl's Grocery around the corner on Mapledale. It was hanging on a hook by the kitchen sink, and it was a big bill. It hadn't been paid for several months.

I knew Mother and Father weren't going to like it, but everything I saw around the house, and everything I had heard for weeks previously, convinced me I had to do it.

Things were somewhat better for our family now. We had moved from the small frame house on Seymour Avenue, across from Noss' Saloon and near Belz's Butcher Shop, into a larger house on West Thirty-ninth Street, off of Archwood Avenue. In this new place we had electricity; no longer did we have to put up, as Mother explained to the neighbors, with foul-smelling oil lamps. We had a much bigger yard, and lots of trees.

Father had sold enough stories to justify this move, but he still was not earning enough to avoid the sharp ups and downs of the irregular arrival of checks from magazines. We were still in a tight place.

At first Father refused flatly to listen to my proposal.

"It would help a whole lot," I urged and, when he smiled, I added, "I could earn five dollars a week. Dogs Marquette told me about a boy who got a job at Lamson's and he is getting five dollars."

"He wants so much to help," I heard Mother tell Father, as they sat one night in the front room.

"I know," Father said, "but it's not right. I wish I had stayed in school. Things would be better for all of us if I had."

I slipped out of the house and went to talk it over with Dogs Marquette, who lived only a short distance from us.

Whenever I had a problem I could count on Herb Marquette. He was fifteen, two years older than I, and big and wise for his age. His nickname came from his three big dogs, one a St. Bernard, a gift from an uncle. Herb was like his St. Bernard, big and gentle, and slow.

Everybody liked him. When he gave his word he kept it. No one could keep a secret better than Dogs.

He was the best friend I had, outside our home. Together we had tramped through Brookside Park. We hopped freight trains in the valley and jumped off at the Eleven Mile Lock on the Ohio Canal during our summer vacations. The only trouble was that once in a while we younger fellows tried to emulate Dogs, not always for our own good—like the time Dogs had a plug of Red Man chewing tobacco.

Just before we swung aboard a B & O boxcar on the way to the Ohio Canal, we all took a bite of his Red Man. Somehow I swallowed mine as I grabbed the iron bar to lift myself up on the train. I got sick, but I didn't want to say so, thinking it would brand me a coward, and I stuck it out.

When we went in swimming off the bridge at the Eleven Mile Lock, I was really sick. Things were blurred, my head ached, my stomach seemed to turn around inside me. I jumped in anyway.

The next thing I knew I was lying flat on my back on the bank by the Canal. Dogs Marquette was standing over me, and the other fellows were around me in a circle.

I opened my eyes.

"What happened?" I asked.

"You got cramps and yelled out," Whitey Richards told me. "Then you went down, and Dogs grabbed you and pulled you out of the water. He really saved you," Whitey said, and we all looked again at Dogs with even greater admiration.

So I went over to Dogs' house that night to talk about leaving school. We sat out on the curb in front of his house. It was May, and warm. The bugs were like a cloud around the street light. They got all over us and we kept brushing them off.

"What do you think, Dogs?" I asked my friend.

"I think you should do it," he said. "You know your Dad needs your help. You can work for a while and then go back to school some time. Right now it's important. I'd do it."

That's all we said. For a long time we just sat on the curb watching the bugs, and occasionally looking up at the stars, until it got late.

"I guess I better go home," I told him.

Mother was waiting for me when I came in, but for once she didn't say anything.

The next morning Father said to me before I left for school, "Son, let's talk about that school question to-night after dinner. Let's get it settled."

That night I waited for Father in his little study to "get it settled." His study was simply a little front room which Mother had ingeniously fixed up, so that Father could have a place of his own in which to write and do his reading and thinking. It was not much, but it was an improvement over the other house where he had sat at the small table in the kitchen. Father had by this time set his back forever on his trade as a carpenter.

It was very quiet in this room. I admired Mother's judgment in choosing it for Father. In the unerring way she always had in such matters, she made the little room literally breathe my father's personality. If at

first sight it seemed cluttered with many miscellaneous
and unrelated articles, closer examination would show
that every solitary one of them had special significance
to Father; each object, however minute or trivial,
was regarded by him as indispensable to his literary
life.

An old oak roll-top desk in the south corner of the
room was the focal point. On it stood his pipe rack,
with his favorite smoke-cured meerschaum, the big can
of his own tobacco mix; over it was his favorite Frederic
Remington landscape of the Old West. A little essay by
Mark Twain and one by Emerson were generally lying
about somewhere. His old red-plaid carpet slippers—
the toe to one worn through—were always, as now, by
his swivel chair, ready to be slipped into the first thing
when he came in to work. The whole room was Father.
It seemed to be a spiritual mirror of him.

Mother had found somewhere a used Woodstock
typewriter. It was old and battered, but she had it
fixed up and it worked. Another improvement for
Father nowadays was writing paper. It still wasn't
manuscript paper; it was the kind we bought for school
in tablet form, but it was better than Mr. Belz's brown
butcher paper. Father seemed to write faster and easier
now.

While I waited for him I looked in the box at the
beginning of his newest story. It was called "The Law
Came to Pecos." He had written eleven pages, and I
was on the last page when Father came in.

"What do you think of it, Louis?" he asked.

"Fine," I said. "It's good, Dad."

He was pleased. "I think this is the best I've ever written, Son, and I hope they take it," he said.

He sat down in the swivel chair.

"Well, Son, let's get at this school business. You're pretty young, you know." He seemed more serious than I had seen him for some time. "Remember, Son, what we decide tonight will have a very important bearing on your whole life."

I nodded. "I understand, Dad."

Running his hand through his great shock of black hair, he said, "I wonder if you really do, Son—that's the trouble. You do seem older than most boys your age— and you understand most things better than they do. But we have to be sure we're doing the right thing."

When he was finally convinced that I had made up my mind, Father got up and put his arm around me, saying, "All right, Son—but let's understand this. We'll go along this way for a while, and if things go good for us, you'll go back to school again one of these days."

We told Mother what we had decided. She looked from one to the other of us and began to cry. Without saying a word, she put the end of her apron to her eyes, and went out. Father watched her go, then sat as if gathering his thoughts.

"Son, sit down. We've made an important decision tonight. Now I want to talk with you. I want you to listen carefully to what I say and remember it for the rest of your life."

He paused for a moment. The room was quiet as a church. Then Father started talking, leaning back in his swivel chair, puffing at his meerschaum pipe.

Son, this is a world of people.

You must always remember that. Life is not simple for people. It is hard. There are very few people in this world whose lot is secure and peaceful and untroubled with cares and worries. It seems that for the privilege of living on this earth most of us must bear some kind of cross.

No two people are alike. That is at once the strength and the weakness of the human race. There are all kinds of people; and they are doing all kinds of things—barbers, lawyers, coal miners, writers (like your Father), ditch-diggers, doctors, thieves, motormen, clerks, policemen—just all kinds of people doing all kinds of things.

A good part of the time people are doing what they want to do; and some of the time, unfortunately, they are doing what the circumstances of life compel them, whether they like it or not, to do.

Whatever you do in life when you grow up, always remember that. If you are doing something in life that you like to do—remember that somebody else may be doing something he doesn't want to do. You may be happy at what you are doing. He may be unhappy doing what he's doing.

Outward appearances are not an infallible measure of people's character. The well-dressed man or woman may be successful by social or economic standards, whereas lacking in qualities of character; and by the same token some man or woman, apparently broken on the wheel of life, may have qualities of character much more desirable and admirable.

The more important thing to look for among people is character. You are apt to find it in the most unexpected places and people.

There is something else to remember. As you grow up there will be many changes in the circumstances of life in this country. Nothing stands still. Right now, as we talk, times are bad. They will be good again. Then they will be bad again; and many people will be out of jobs, and the country will be in a turmoil.

There will be wars and panics, and troubles of one kind or another.

There always have been. There always will be. In everything that you do, in everything you think, always, remember that people are more important than any other considerant in the world. People make the world. The world does not make people.

Remember, also, that because a man is not, by the measure of this world, recognized as a success it does not follow that he is a failure. Too many times it will be found that men of comparable abilities in like fields of work will turn out differently, because circumstances favor one and not the other.

Each man, however, should make the utmost of what nature has given him. There is no excuse for failure there.

Everything I have said to you tonight means this: People are, after all, the most precious, fascinating, important, useful, vexatious, and yet indispensable beings in the world.

You will have one life. It will be lived, every minute of it, with other people. They will be restless, irritable, kindly, serene, helpful, inconsiderate, mean, good, as people always have been, and, perhaps, as they always will be. But they are really good deep down inside— and that's where you should look to find them.

Father stood up. He had talked a long time. I had never listened so closely to anything before. Somehow I knew this was important—very important to me.

"We better get to bed now, Son, it's getting late," he said. "And some day, when I get a chance, I'll write out for you what we've been talking about tonight." He kept his promise, and I have written it here as he wrote it then.

I was almost asleep that night when Father came in,

shook me gently and said, "Son, I forgot to give you something."

The object Father handed me shone brightly in a shaft of light from the hall. It was Grandpa Lucien's watch, the one he was given by his own father when he went away to the Civil War. It was the one thing I longed most to have, and Father knew it.

"I just thought that a young man who is making a very important decision for himself and his parents ought to have something important to remember it by," he said. He patted my head, and walked out of the bedroom.

It was a long time before I finally went to sleep, with Grandpa Lucien's watch in my hand.

Chapter 5

T HERE WAS only one job I wanted, if I had
my choice. That was on one of the newspapers.
I wanted more than anything else in the world
to be a reporter—to write—to cover big events—to see
the police and fire stories as they really happened, instead of just reading about them.

When Father's first story was published, a reporter
and a photographer were sent out to our house on Seymour Avenue.

I listened to the interview and watched, fascinated, as
the photographer set up his tripod, screwed his camera
on top of it, put a black hood over it, filled a tray with
flashlight powder, and posed Father and Mother on
the flowered davenport in our small living room. The
flash went off with a big boom, and a heavy cloud of

smoke filled the whole house. Mother had to open all the doors to get it out.

I asked the reporter every question I could think of about the newspaper business. He was a tall, good-looking young man, and to me he seemed a great adventurer, a man who lived in another world—a world of romance and tragedy and history, where things of importance were always happening—and where he was always present. That was where I wanted to be.

Father suggested that I try The Leader. "You know where it is?" he asked.

"Yes, Dad, I know," I said. "I think I can find it."

"It's a long way to walk, and I guess there is no other way to get there right now," he said. "It must be better than four miles. Do you think you can make it after school?"

"I'll go right from school, Dad," I said.

I was happy and he saw it in my face.

"Mother, I think no matter what happens we've lost a schoolboy in our family and acquired a young man," Father said.

I couldn't keep my mind on school that day. Dancing around in it was a kaleidoscope of pictures—a newspaper office—reporters—writers—big presses—noise and excitement and lots of action.

When the final bell rang, I couldn't get out of the building fast enough. I ran down West Twenty-fifth Street, and then caught myself, thinking, *better slow down, you've got a long way to go and you can't run the whole distance.* Besides that, I told myself, I ought to be calm enough to talk sensibly when I got to the

Paco Building on Superior Avenue where The Leader was put out.

It was a long walk. I hitched a ride on the back end of an ice wagon for part of the way. After that, a man in a wagon loaded with furniture motioned to me, asking, "Want a lift across the bridge, Sonny?"

He looked like a nice man, fat, good-natured, and accommodating, so I climbed up on his wagon.

"Where are you headed for, Sonny?"

"I'm going to The Leader to get a job," I said, and just saying it made me feel big and important.

"So," he said. "What kind of a job you going to get?"

"Well, I don't know," I said. "I guess I'll take any kind of a job I can get. I'd like to be a reporter, though."

"You're kind of young to be a reporter, aren't you?"

"I'm almost thirteen," I said.

The big, fat man turned his attention to his horse, as the bridge lifted for a river boat.

"The Leader is just on the other side of this bridge," he said. "I just hope, Sonny, you get that job. I wish I had got a job like that when I was your age." He pulled up his wagon in front of a building and pointed at it. "There it is, Sonny."

After he said, "Giddy-yap," to his horse and started moving away, he looked back, and I did, too. We waved at each other, and his big face with its beaming smile gave me just the courage I needed to go inside and try for my first real job.

It was dark inside the front door. There was only a

faint light from the ceiling. An elevator came creaking down to the ground floor, with the man who ran it pulling on a cable. It was open all around except for iron bars with a design like a big flower at the front.

When I got in, the sour-faced operator snapped out at me, "What floor do you want?"

"I don't know—the floor where the City Editor is," I said, feeling my courage sink.

On the way up he didn't say a word. Neither did I.

"Over there," he directed, when the elevator reached the third floor. The sign on the door ahead said: "Editorial Offices." Cautiously I pushed it open and slipped inside.

I wasn't prepared for the sight that met my eyes. I thought it would be a small office with the City Editor sitting at a desk. Instead, it was a big office, the biggest one I had ever seen. There were many people in it, all rushing around. Typewriters were clattering. People were shouting. Men and boys were running from one desk to another. I stood paralyzed just inside the door. It opened again behind me and I jumped hastily out of the way as a big man came in.

"What can I do for you, Son?" he asked in a surprisingly gentle, low voice.

He was rather stout, his hair touched with gray.

"Sir, I came to see the City Editor about a job," I said, and after I got the words out sweat broke out all over me.

"All right, Son, I'll take you over to him," the man said. "What's your name?" he asked.

I told him. He looked at me again.

"That's a familiar name," he said. "There's a Charles Alden Seltzer who writes short stories. Are you related to him?"

I was never more proud. Here, in a big newspaper office, someone knew my father. Suddenly all my courage came back.

"Yes, sir, he's my father," I said.

"My name is Slayton—Victor Slayton," the man said. "I write editorials for this paper. I met your father once." He put his hand on my shoulder. "Come on along with me, Son—and I'll introduce you to the City Editor. His bark is worse than his bite."

Overwhelmed, and yet fascinated, by the noise and confusion, I went with Victor Slayton to the far end of the crowded room.

"Sam, here's a young man who has come in looking for a job," Mr. Slayton said.

The City Editor wore a green eye shade and glasses. He was big and redheaded, and to me he looked definitely unfriendly. I remembered Mr. Slayton's comment that his bark was worse than his bite, but the minute I saw him I was scared.

"He looks like a good boy to me, Sam," said Mr. Slayton, patting me on the shoulder and walking away.

"Well, young man, what is it?" the City Editor asked.

"Sir, I want to be a newspaper reporter," I said, and then quickly added, "I would like any kind of a job that you have open—any kind."

Under the grim face I thought there was a faint smile.

"We haven't any jobs open for reporters," he said.

"And you're just a little too young for that kind of a job. We might have a job for you, though—a job as office boy. The work is hard. The hours are long. It's a tough job. It doesn't pay much. We could give you $3.25 a week."

He watched me closely. I couldn't believe my luck. Everything was happening just right for me—Mr. Slayton coming in behind me at the door and knowing my father—getting the very kind of a job I wanted at the first place I tried.

Sam Anson, the City Editor, brought me up sharply.

"Do you want it?"

"I do—I do—I do," I said, repeating myself so rapidly that, in spite of himself, he smiled.

"All right, when can you come to work?" he asked.

"Right now, sir," I said.

"That's fine, but not necessary," he said. "You come to work—let's see," he said, looking at the calendar by his desk. "You come to work next Wednesday—the first of the month. This is a morning paper. We start our day at noon. You report to me at noon—and no telling when you'll leave."

I thanked him and reached out my hand to shake his, but he had already turned to someone else at his desk.

I went over to a corner where I saw Mr. Slayton sitting at a desk.

"I got a job as an office boy," I told him. "And I'm supposed to start next Wednesday morning. I just wanted to thank you, sir."

Mr. Slayton invited me to sit down. He asked about

Father. He wanted to know how far I was in school, and why I was leaving.

"It's too bad you can't finish your schooling, Son, because later in life I am afraid you're going to miss it, especially in this business," he said. "However, if you have to leave school, don't ever let it worry you. You'll have to work twice as hard as other people to make up for it though. Do you like good books?"

I told Mr. Slayton that Father had fixed up a program for my reading way back when I was a small boy.

"That couldn't be too many years ago, could it?" he asked, with a smile.

"It seems a long time ago to me," I answered, very seriously.

"This job is a pretty tough one, Son," he said. "You'll do errands for a lot of people around here; and sometimes they'll shout and scream at you. You'll have to learn to take a lot, and keep smiling."

I walked slowly out of the big, noisy room. This, I thought, is where I will work. These are the people—this is the newspaper office I had dreamed about almost since I could remember. It was the first time I had ever been in one, and it wasn't quite like I had imagined it. It was bigger, noisier, more confused, disorderly, and dirty. But I liked it. It thrilled and excited me. The only thing I regretted, as I walked out of the City Room toward the elevator, was that my first day at work seemed so far away.

On the way home I didn't get a lift; I walked all the way, but the distance seemed short. I couldn't wait to tell Father and Mother. The last half mile I ran.

Sunday passed so slowly, it made me nervous. That was always a day for rest in our house. Mother saw to that. She also saw to it that we got all fixed up for Sunday School, something she insisted upon even when our clothes were patched and frayed—as, in the earlier days, on Seymour Avenue, they frequently were. It was not uncommon for us to wear pants and shirts and underclothes made over from those worn out by either Father, Grandpa Lucien, or Uncle Ray. But we went to Sunday School, come bad weather or good, little food or poor clothes—so persistently, in fact, that Father once said, "Ella, I believe you'd send these children to Sunday School dressed like they were in the Garden of Eden."

This Sunday morning Mother brushed my hair, and, had I permitted it, she would have shined my shoes. I expect she was thinking how soon now I would be grown up and away from her care.

"I want you to be shined and polished up this morning," she said. "And when you bow your head in prayer at Sunday School today, you thank God for the wonderful opportunity he has given you."

I thought Monday morning would never come. I wanted to get up, go to school, and tell my teacher, Miss Money, all about my job. I lay in bed going over and over in my mind what I would say to her. She had been my favorite teacher, except for Miss Effie Pekar, but even so I was a little afraid of her.

Father said to me at breakfast, "Son, would you want me to go up to school some time today and explain to Miss Money why you are leaving?"

"No, Dad," I said quickly, "I want to tell her myself."

One thing that made it easier was the fact that Miss Money was leaving herself in about a month, to be principal at another school. The afternoon she had broken the news to us, the whole class cried, including even Dogs Marquette. We would never get another teacher like Miss Money.

"You will like the new teacher," she assured us.

"No, no, no," the whole class shouted in unison.

Whitey Richards, who had really caused Miss Money more headaches than anybody else, got up and said, between sobs, "We'll never forget you, Miss Money—never."

The rest of the class took up Whitey's words, and we began to chant, "We'll never forget Miss Money—we'll never forget Miss Money—NEVER, NEVER!"

And we never did.

"I don't think we ever forget a good teacher," Father said, when I told him about it.

As I started to school for the last time, I met up with Dogs Marquette, Whitey Richards, Orin Canfield, and a bunch of the other fellows in my class, just as we were passing Miss Money's house on Archwood Avenue. It was a big house, set well back from the street, in the midst of flowering quince and apple trees. We came to a stop in front of it, paying a sort of silent tribute, I suppose, to the teacher who was leaving us.

I thought how many times I had delivered the afternoon paper there. Miss Money always liked for me to lay the paper down carefully on the large porch which stretched across the whole front of the house, but I rarely got to do it. She was almost always at the door when I came up the steps. Sometimes she would wave at me through the window.

She let me pick apples and quinces for my mother when they were in season. It was always hard for me to tell about quinces, because they seemed to look and taste, when they were supposed to be ripe, just the way they did when they were green. Miss Money would say:

"I can never remember whether you mother likes quinces, Louis, but you take some anyway because they do make such wonderful jelly."

Occasionally I would run an errand for Miss Money, to the hardware store, or the apothecary shop, and sometimes to Mr. Corlett's grocery on West Thirty-third Street, right around the corner from where she lived. For this she always gave me candy, always the same kind—a delicious chocolate cream. I never saw them in any store, and I supposed she made them herself. She gave me only one, handing it to me on a small piece of white paper. I always tried to make it last, and it never did.

"We'll miss her, all right," Orin said. "Did you fellows know anything about it, before she told us?"

We didn't. We were surprised as much as he was, we said.

Dogs turned to me, and whispered, "They're going to get another surprise, aren't they? Are you still going through with it?"

"Yes, Dogs, I've got a job," I told him. "I'm going to work on Wednesday."

I didn't tell him where. I wanted him to ask because I was proud of the answer.

"Where you going to work?" he asked.

"I'm going to be office boy at The Leader," I told him, and then, in a rush of ambition, I added, "And someday I'm going to be a star reporter. I'm going to—"

I realized how foolish and young I sounded when Dogs put his hand on my shoulder.

"Can I tell these fellows?" he asked.

"Maybe I better tell Miss Money first," I said.

All morning I tried to get a chance to tell her, but she was too busy. At recess, she walked right out of the classroom to the principal's office, and she didn't come back until the school bell rang.

At the end of the afternoon I waited around after everybody else went out. The classroom was very quiet. Miss Money sat working at her desk. I found I didn't know how to tell her after all. All the words I had planned so carefully, I forgot.

She looked up. "Well, Louis—is something wrong?"

When I didn't say anything, she got up. She was small and trim, dressed as usual in a black skirt and a gray blouse, her black hair done up in a round bun on top of her head.

When she sat at her desk going over our papers, she wore big round glasses with shiny metal around them. I liked her better without the glasses because they seemed to make her look stern. As she walked toward me, she saw me looking at them and took them off. When she did, her whole appearance seemed to change. The quiet, gentle expression came back to her face, and her bright, kind eyes reassured me.

"We're all sorry you're going to leave, Miss Money," I said, trying to cover up my nervousness.

"I am, too, Louis," Miss Money said, and smiled at me, adding, "But that's not why you stayed after school, is it—just to tell me that?"

"No, Miss Money," I said. "It's something else."

"Is it something very serious?" she asked, sitting down in the seat at the desk ahead of mine.

"Yes, Miss Money, it is." I stopped for a bit, trying to find the right words, finally adding, "It is for *me*, Miss Money."

"You're having a little difficulty telling me, Louis," she said. "Why don't you just tell me—right out. What is it?"

"Well," I said, "I am leaving school, too." Then I hurried on. "I have a job, Miss Money, as an office boy at The Leader. I start next Wednesday. I'll have to get all my things out of my desk tonight and get my report card. And I have to have a note from you and the principal so I can give it to Mr. Anson—he's the City Editor at The Leader. He's the man I'm going to work for."

Miss Money looked at me for a long moment without saying a word. I felt uncomfortable.

"But, Louis, you're so young to be going to work," she said. "So young to be leaving school. It doesn't seem right."

To take the finality out of it, I said, "I might come back sometime, Miss Money, if things get better at home; or maybe, if I don't keep my job."

She almost snapped at me. "Louis, don't talk that way —of course you'll keep your job. Of course you'll make good at it." My eyes must have shone in response, for she said, "Now, that's better. You must never say that again. You will always make good at whatever you do. Always remember that."

I nodded.

"This is something I never expected," Miss Money said. "I always imagined that you would go right on through school, to high school, and perhaps even to college. Louis, I am really sorry to see you go."

As she said it, tears came to my eyes. I was very close at that moment to changing my mind.

"I can't say that you've been one of my best pupils," she said. "And I can't say you have been the best-behaved boy in the class. You have done your share of the mischief around here, and I am not sure that I caught you at all you were responsible for."

In my heart I knew that there were many resource-fully executed maneuvers in which my part was not a wholly incidental one. Dogs Marquette's image jumped into my mind when she said this, and for some strange reason, I remembered how small Miss Money looked when Dogs stood beside her at the desk while she was giving it to him for some prank he had led us all into. I couldn't hide a smile, and Miss Money quickly went on.

"Well, we won't go into that now—we'll let bygones be bygones."

I was willing.

71

"I suppose you know that this is a big step you are taking."

I liked to hear Miss Money talk. Her voice was rich and low and quiet, her words always well-chosen and clear.

"You might come back some time when family matters are cleared up," she said. "Perhaps not. You really are a good boy. You try to do the right thing. That's the most important thing of all, isn't it?"

I didn't quite know whether Miss Money expected me to answer her. Before I had time to make up my mind she went on.

"I only hope that wherever you are, or whatever you do, you will always try to improve yourself," she said. "Look for the principles and ideals you think are the good ones, and keep to them, fight for them, make them your own. Be a good boy, and make me proud that I was your teacher."

I got up to go. Miss Money put her hand in mine.

"Goodbye, Louis, and good luck," she said. "I believe in you."

I ducked my head to get my belongings from my desk, but really to keep Miss Money from seeing the tears in my eyes. She suspected as much, for she patted me on the back and returned to her own desk. I left the classroom, not even stopping to take a last look.

The whole thing hit me suddenly. It was going to be tough to leave school. Until now I had been more interested in my job, and the adventure before me. Now I realized that I would not go to Lincoln High School —nor to college. I would not have a chance to be a great student, or a star athlete. The door behind me was securely locked, and I was out in a different life.

I didn't go home right away. I walked down the broken path into Brookside Park, and gradually my mood changed. A fellow can't go to school forever. He has to leave some time. I was just leaving earlier than the rest. And I was going to the best job a fellow could have, and a job that would help my mother and father.

And with that comforting thought, I walked back up the hill and toward home—putting school behind me, and my new job ahead of me.

Chapter 6

"**H**ANG YOUR CAP over here," Big Ed directed me, pointing to a coat rack in the corner that was used by the office boys. Big Ed Huneker was eighteen and had been there for two years. He knew his way around. He was not only head office boy, but he was the boss, and he knew it.

I had been on my job for only ten minutes, and already, in Big Ed, I had run against my first problem. I determined that no matter what he said or did I would go along with him on it. I was willing to overlook anything.

Big Ed showed me around, pointing out who everybody was and telling me what I was supposed to do. I made a list.

"What's the matter, can't you remember anything?" he demanded.

"Yes, but I just want to be sure," I said.

Somebody shouted, "Boy! Boy!"

Big Ed said to me, "Go over and see what he wants. On the double!"

The man on what Big Ed told me was the copy desk was holding up a sheet of paper.

"Composing room, in a hurry," he said. I didn't know where that was. Big Ed hadn't told me. As I hesitated, a short, fat, bald-headed man looked up from the next desk.

"Lost, kid?" he asked, smiling. "Here, I'll show you the way. You'll have to learn sometime. You're new, aren't you? What's your name?"

I told him. He repeated it, laughing.

"That's good," he said. "Seltzer—Bromo Seltzer. That's your name, is it? That's good, Bromo Seltzer."

When we got to the composing room, he showed me around, and introduced me—always as "Bromo Seltzer."

I learned that his name was Henry Walter, and that he handled "wire" news. Everybody called him "Hank." He became a good friend as time went on, but he fastened a nickname on me that first day which has lasted through almost all my newspaper life, and still crops up now and again in many places.

From noon until dark I was kept busy, rushing everywhere. I filled paste pots, ran copy, went after sandwiches and beer, carried big, heavy canvas mailbags from the Post Office two blocks away. In the late afternoon, the Make-up Editor sent me down to the pressroom in the basement of the building, carrying a batch of white sheets with lines and numbers on them. I didn't know what they were, but the pressroom foreman snatched them from me and instantly started to pass along instructions. I could hardly tear myself away, but I knew I had to keep jumping.

About seven o'clock, when Big Ed said it was time for me to eat, I headed straight back to the pressroom, and crept into a dark corner behind long rows of big rolls of paper. It smelled good—the paper and the ink. In the light around the presses I could see men working. They had on overalls and paper hats shaped like boxes.

Nobody bothered me. I was all alone. And I had a front-row seat at the show I wanted more than anything else in the world to see. The paper would be coming out pretty soon. I had learned already that the bulldog edition went to press at 7:45 o'clock. It was almost that now, as I sat in the dark corner watching the men "dressing" the presses under the lights—absent-mindedly eating the banana Mother had put in my box lunch.

A loud bell rang. Switches were thrown. The big presses started. They began to thunder. The paper started to roll through them. The roar increased, and the basement began to shake. My heart began to pound, as I sat forward, straining my eyes to watch.

Now I knew, at last, I was in the newspaper business: down here where the presses were rolling with voices of thunder; and upstairs, on the third floor, where I was an office boy now, and would be something more— I wasn't sure what—as the future spread ahead.

I went back upstairs to work. It was an exciting evening. The paper put out an extra on a big fire, and I watched, absorbed, the process of getting a newspaper together under pressure—bringing in a big story, writing it, setting it up, putting it on the presses and rolling away with it.

I got home the next morning at five o'clock. The sun was just peeking up over the horizon when I walked wearily up the front steps of our house. The day before I had got up at daybreak as usual, and the time had seemed endless until noon when I reported for work. I had wondered what I would do from daybreak to noon every day. I knew now. I would be fast asleep, and I doubted whether I would wake up in time to report to work at noon.

But I did. I was on my first job and I loved it. I knew already that I would never go back to school. I was out in another world—the world of roaring presses, which I had longed for from the time I was a very small boy, and which I would love for the rest of my life with ever increasing strength and devotion. I was in the greatest, the most exciting, the most satisfying business on the face of the earth.

Many things were to happen—many of them unexpected, hard, and discouraging, elevating to the summits one moment and plunging to the deep valleys of despair the next. It is a severe, sometimes brutal business, a dedicated, selfless business, a business woven inextricably with life—a business which is life itself.

Six months after I went to work at The Leader, I wrote my first story—the one that helped me, at almost fourteen, win my first promotion.

I was on my way from the old City Hall with some copy that Billy Corrigan had written. To get back to The Leader I had to pass through the Public Square.

Just as I reached the Square an old, open-sided street-car hit a Burns & Bowie Pie Wagon, drawn by a couple of dapple-gray horses. The streetcar in turning had hit the pie wagon with such force that it split it almost apart. Burns & Bowie's best pies of all varieties and colors spattered the Public Square. It was a mess, but a colorful mess. People were picking up the pies, laughing, and having a lot of fun. Some boys were happily cramming down pie as if they were in a pie-eating contest at a picnic.

I knew it was a story. I also knew that I had Billy Corrigan's City Hall copy to get to The Leader on time. What was I to do? I spotted a Postal Telegraph messenger standing at the curb, watching the catastrophe, and rushed over to him, saying, "I'll give you twenty-five cents if you will take this envelope three blocks to The Leader."

The Postal Telegraph boy was older than I. He looked at me as if to say, "Why don't you do it yourself?" But he looked even more closely at the quarter. He took it, and also the envelope, while I gave him the directions to the City Editor's desk in the Paco Building.

I then went over to the policeman who was in charge. When I told him that I was from The Leader, he looked at me, and smiled in unbelief.

"What's your name, Son?" he asked.

"My name is Seltzer, and I am a reporter," I told him,

more boldly than I had ever said anything to anyone before.

Perhaps even then he didn't believe me; but he did answer a few questions I asked, and I got the names of the people involved and other facts.

"Where is the man who was driving the pie wagon?" I asked the policeman.

"Right over there," he pointed.

I went over to the driver, and from him got an inventory of what his wagon was carrying when it was hit by the streetcar.

"Where is the motorman of the streetcar?" was my next question. After answering me, the policeman added, "Son, you ask a lot of questions."

I went over to the motorman, and from him got a firsthand description of how it felt to spray the Public Square with a large batch of Burns & Bowie pies.

Then I went back to The Leader office. The instant I walked in I knew I was in trouble. Mr. Anson glowered at me.

"Where have you been—and what do you mean sending a Postal Telegraph messenger here with copy you are supposed to deliver yourself?"

I waited until his wrath had run down somewhat, and then I explained. He listened, and he was interested.

"Should I give this to somebody, Mr. Anson?" I asked.

"No, no," he said, shortly. "Sit down and write it yourself."

It was fortunate for me that I had practiced on Father's battered old Woodstock. I sat down at a vacant desk and spent a long time writing the story. Big Ed Huneker didn't help any. He kept coming around making nasty remarks, naturally furious because I had been given the chance to write the story. He had been on the paper for two and a half years—as compared with my six months—and he hadn't written anything as yet.

I finished the story, and took it over to Mr. Anson. As he read it, he used his big black pencil on it, taking a word out here, and putting one in there. He looked up.

"Bromo," he said, "that's a nice little story. We'll use it just the way you wrote it."

Two things happened the next day. I proudly showed Father and Mother the front page of The Leader with my pie story—and my name on it—the first by-line of my newspaper career. I also went home at dinner-time, instead of eating my lunch in the dark, exciting recesses of the pressroom, to tell them I had been promoted.

Chapter 7

THANKS TO the accident to Burns & Bowie's
pies, I was moved into the Sunday Department
of The Leader, to write a weekly column for
the Metropolitan Section under a by-line thought up
by my new boss, Chester Hope. The by-line, which
was also the name of the column, was: By Louie, The
Office Boy. It was generally printed "Luee, The Offis
Boy," since the column featured as many misspellings
as I could manage to invent. That sort of thing seemed
funnier in 1911 than it does today.

"Luee" was to take me to many interesting places
during the next few months. I covered dance halls, cir-
cuses and carnivals, symphony orchestras, police stations, hospitals, and many other places, some unsavory,
but not many.

My problem now was to get people to take me seriously. I was going on fourteen. I felt grown up; I no longer thought about school. But I looked as young as I was, and nothing I tried seemed to make me look any older. Sometimes it was hard to get into the places I was supposed to go.

Most boys my age wore knickers and stockings. I wore long pants. In a picture I had seen of Kipling he had on a big, black bow tie. I bought one for eight cents at May's on the Public Square, thinking it would make me look older. It didn't. I even tried growing a mustache. Nothing happened. The fuzz was the same color as my hair, which was so blond that some people called me Whitey.

My problem wasn't helped by the sketches they printed to illustrate my column, which showed me with a big batch of hair flying in all directions, the big, black bow tie (which I began to wear all the time), and a Buster Brown collar which made me look like Little Lord Fauntleroy—the one character in the world I most abhorred. I was always sketched in some kind of action. If I was writing about a dance hall, I was shown skidding desperately across the floor; if at a circus, hanging on for dear life with one hand, a frightened look on my face.

I hated the sketches sometimes, because they made me look so young and, I thought, so much like a sissy. I knew I wasn't very big. I was only five feet, five inches tall, and rather skinny—and that made it all the worse. However, I dared not say anything about it to my boss, Chester Hope. He might, I was afraid—a chill going down my spine even at the thought—take the column out altogether.

"I want the column and the sketches to make you look like a wide-eyed boy to whom all the experiences you write about are new and wonderful and exciting," he said.

That was not hard because they were. I enjoyed my work, and I was proud of the reporter's badge in my pants pocket. It was in the form of a five-pointed star, made of very light metal, with an inscription in big black letters: "Reporter for The Leader," with my number—No. 26. The badges were changed each year, because they sometimes got lost and fell into the wrong hands. Once a robber talked his way into a downtown store and got away with $500 from a cash register by flashing a reporter's badge. I felt a personal sense of relief when he was caught.

When I had trouble getting into a place, I showed my badge, but it didn't always help.

"Nobody's sending a kid like you over here," a big hard-jawed doorman told me one day. I was trying to get backstage at the Hippodrome Theater to see Sarah Bernhardt, who was in Cleveland on one of her "final" American tours.

"But I am a reporter," I insisted stubbornly.

"Out!" he said, sharply.

I tried to argue with him, but he wouldn't listen.

"Please have someone call my office," I said finally. "They'll tell you. I'm doing a story for The Sunday Leader. My name is Louie Seltzer. I write the Luee, The Offis Boy column."

83

He looked down at me from well above six feet. "You Louie?" he demanded, a sarcastic tinge in his tone.

"Yes," I said, sounding tougher than I was because I was both angry and worried.

"Well, why didn't you tell me? How was I to know? You a reporter!" he added, unbelieving. "Well, they sure pick 'em young, don't they? Yep, there's that tie. All right, go on in."

I went backstage, where Sarah Bernhardt was rehearsing with Lou Tellegen. He was a tall, nice-looking man, then very young and, at this moment, impatient. He even spoke sharply to Miss Bernhardt, but she silenced him by simply looking at him.

Miss Bernhardt turned the tables on me. She interviewed me instead of the other way around, asking me many questions, about myself, about Cleveland, about our paper.

When I got back to the office, I reported to Howard Denby, the assistant Sunday Editor, under whom I worked directly. He was a small man who disappeared behind big glasses, and was handicapped by a limp and a little stutter. But he was lively, very lively. He always had ideas, and everybody seemed to come to him looking for them.

"Wonderful," Howard Denby said, when I told him that Miss Bernhardt had asked most of the questions. "Write it that way, Louie—Sarah Bernhardt Interviews Luee, The Offis Boy."

I did, and that's the way it ran. It had a sketch of

Sarah Bernhardt with a pencil and pad taking down notes, while I sat on a big throne-like chair as if I were somebody important. Even I had to laugh at the sketch when Van Orsdale, the artist, showed it to Howard Denby and me.

"But what will Miss Bernhardt say?" I asked.

Howard Denby said, "She'll be more pleased with that than a dozen other pieces or pictures."

If I had a copy of that Bernhardt column, I would reprint it here, but somehow in the clutter of forty years of clippings, it has failed to survive. She *was* pleased. From Detroit she wrote asking for the original of Van Orsdale's sketch, and in her note she complimented me for the unusual way the story was handled. Howard Denby was really responsible and, while I had always admired him, after that my respect for him was unlimited. I tried to follow his every suggestion.

Sometimes his assignments had a touch of inspired fantasy. One day I remember I was told to go over to see the mayor and find out—not something about city politics—but how to skin the cat. The interview ended up that day with me flat on the floor and the mayor doing acrobatics between two office chairs. This is the way my column ran.

> Tweet, tweet, tweet.
> I looked outen under th' bed clothes an' there wuz a robin hangin' on th' eaves-trough twitterin' to beat Sousa's band. Well, I knew it wuz time for me to get my duds on an' beat it downstairs, an' eat breakfast an' go to work. Somethin' inside o' me kept sayin' that I wuz to do somethin' great today—this is Tuesday.

I jist got to work about two seconds afore th' Boss comes in with a new spring suit an' a harmonizin' colorful tie. The boss sez, "Mornin', Ach Luee."

"Say, Luee, this mornin' you make an appointment with Mayer Baker an' ask him how to skin-th'-cat," he goes on.

Holy hemlocks—go over to the city hall an' ask th' mayer how to skin a cat. I didn't want to ask him, so I sed, "Why, boss, I know how to skin 'em. Jist take mother's great big bread knife and slit their squeakers an' then rip an' rip."

"No, no, no—I mean exercise. Skin-th'-cat off th' limb of a tree or with gym paraphernalia. You know he got out in his back yard last Sunday an' showed th' Mayer, Jr., Jack, how to skin it at his home on Crawford avenue."

Well, I went upstairs an' got some soap an' a scrubbin' brush an' a comb and a whisk broom an' started to get redy for th' catastrophe. Then I went downstairs an' had my shoes shined an' I looked like a real sport.

"Is Mr. Baker in, I want to ask him how to skin-th'-cat."

"Billy" Murphy, th' mayer's secretary, looked at me kind uv dazed like, an' then let out a whoop like an Iroquoee Injun gettin' redy to scalp a pale face. Then I began wonderin' whether th' Boss wuz tryin' to string me an' I was jist goin' to beat it out when th' Mayer comes outen his offis an' looks at me an' sez, "Come in."

"Why -er, I—I c-come over to-o a-ask ya how ya' skin-th'-cat th' rite way?"

Then that famous smile of his spread all over th' place an' he sez, "So youre Luee, The Offis Boy." I sez yes, an' he smiled laconically.

Well, he took off his hat 'n' his coat an' got down in th' middle of his offis an' sez, "Now watch me." He got down on his han's an' knees an' pulled two chairs over to th' center an' sent a fellow out fer a piece of railin' an' then he laid th' railin' across th' tops of th' two chairs an' I held one side an' th' fellow held th' other

an' th' mayer skinned-th'-cat. First he skinned it front
wards, then he skinned it backwards and then he
skinned it sidewise an' then he said "Well, I'm all
tuckered out, Luee. Ya' see I haven't done this fer over
twenty-five years or so an' I've lost all of my supple-
ness."

Then I got down an' started skinnin' it an' I went
kerplunk on th' floor an' "Billy" Murphy rushed in an'
thought that I had assassinated th' mayer an' it looked
that way some how—the way he wuz standin' there
gaspin' fer breath with his coat off an' his glasses layin'
on th' floor an' his hair all ruffled up, but he gasped,
"T-t-t's nothin', Billy. I'm jist showin' Luee how to
skin-th'-cat." Billy winked at th' mayer an' he winked
back an' Billy looked back an' 'twas all over.

The mayer an' me got to talkin' of when I first
started in as a Offis Boy an' I kin remember now the
"fatherly advice" he gave me concernin' how to work
an' when to work an' not let th' other fell-ow do th'
work. Fer two years I worked an' th' Mayer has always
kept in touch with me an' told me what to do an'
everything I shouldn't do. I used to read Dead Eye Pete
stories with yellow covers, but I don't no more cause he
found out when I went over to see him skin-th'-cat.

After workin' as a Offis Boy fer two years an' writin'
about dances an' seein' that the scouts were made
known, I got a chance to see Mayer Baker skin-th'-cat,
but I'm tellin' you truthfully that th' way he skinned
it wasn't th' way that I would have skinned wun if he
hadn't showed me how.

He, he! Fer the last two months I've been sittin'
aroun' th' offis readin' yellow-back literature an' my
forehead is gettin' all wrinkled up when I get excited
an' th' hero comes in an' dispels my fear of havin' th'
heroine thrown over a 1,ooo-foot precipice by a half-
breed. Mayer Baker made me promise that I wouldn't
ever take an' read one of those stories with "Blood an'
Thunder" in 'em again.

He'z goin' censor all th' stuff I read. Some honor to

hev a mayer o.k. your readin' matter, but he better o.k. th' stuff my dad rites. It ain't blood an' thunder but it's just as interestin' an' excitin'.

Ghee! I wunder what th' mayer'll do, I s'pose he'll get a bunch of books fer me to read so they'll last me until he gits back from Your-Up, Huh? Well, jist watch Dead-Eye Pete, Red Nose Mike, Tommy th' Cracksman, Tamale Pete, th' Mexican Greaser, Snaky Loop Ike, Ace, th' Cowboy Pote, Two Gun Harlan, Norton, th' Range Boss, an' Split-'em-Open Jim get busy wen th' mayer's boat leaves fer Your-Up.

Guess I'll skin-th'-cat before I kin go to sleep—or throw a shoe at 'm.

Miss Bernhardt was the most wonderful theater personage I met that year—or ever—but there were others. I wrote up Donald Brian one night under the headline:

Luee Shows up 'Cowboy' Donald Brian
Ropes Chorus Girls on Stage

The accompanying sketch showed me in complete cowboy regalia, and I had plenty to say about the inaccuracies of the costume Donald wore. Various bits of imaginary horseplay with members of the cast rounded out the story.

As I wuz sayin', afore I described Percy, he cums up behind me an' gives me a shove an' sent me a whirlin' outen th' stage an' Donald grabbed me by th' collar an' pulls me back again. All durin' th' intermisshun after Don an' Percy left me ta' dress fer th' third act, May DeSousa an' me had a nice chat, an' every once in a while Cissie Sewell would talk awhile an' then go back again to th' glimmerin' footlites.

When May found out it wuz time fer her act I spied a little chorus girl jist about my size an'—"whoop—ee—

e—ee," she winked at me an' a little smile lit up her face an'—"Aw, ghee, quit yure kiddin' kid," an' she turned aroun' an' sed, "Sit down, yure rockin' th' boat," an' jist as she sez that I went kerplunk into a nice soft Morris chair an' she set down in ut with me, an' then another wun came in an' set down on th' other side. Cissie sed, 'Come on out with me, Luee, and dance." I did, but not outen th' stage.

Well, th' big seen, with Donald an' Cissie, wuz on, an' then I had nearly evry chorus girl in th' comp'ny sittin' or tryin' to sit in thet chair with me, an' I was tryin' ta solve "why boys leave home," but ta' save my buckskin hide I couldn't. Well, th' show bein' over, Don comes runnin' off th' stage, an' so does Cissie, and they both grabs my arms and marches me off the stage, an' then Cissie left too an' I went into Don's dressin' room with him, and he doffs his stage costume an' takes th' red paint off his face an' gets a pair of boxin' gloves an' puts them on me, an' sez, "Awright, Luee, let 'er rip," . . .

One morning, not long after the Bernhardt "interview," I arrived at the office and pitched my cap neatly over the hall tree from a dozen paces away. I liked that trick, which I had acquired by long practice. But my cap didn't stay there long that morning.

Howard Denby saw me and called out, "Got a job for you, Louie. Put the cap back on, and come on over."

That assignment led to the most important personal event in my whole life.

Chapter 8

THE ASSIGNMENT was simple, but interesting. I was to accompany a couple of young movie stars on their tour of personal appearances in a half dozen picture houses. First I was directed to meet them at their hotel and spend some time with them before they started out, to see how they lived, what they ate, how they were dressed. Then I had to follow them around to various social functions.

The movie-house appearances were scheduled for the evening. The first was on Madison Avenue, on the West Side, and it was in my own neighborhood, only two blocks from where I lived.

A big crowd was milling around in front of the theater, and the manager was waiting for us at the door. He led us down the aisle toward the stage, apologizing

for the fact that we would have to cross the stage to get
to the dressing room, but obviously enjoying the attention of the huge, waiting audience.

"Dressing room" was a grand name for it. It was only
a small tent pitched at the other side of the stage. In it
the demure little stars—teen-age sisters who dressed
alike—were to get into the costumes they had worn
in their last picture.

I led the way across the dim stage. In the darkened
theater, there was only a single, small square of light,
and by some compulsive force my eyes focused there.
Looking up at me, deep into my very heart and soul,
were two large, luminous brown eyes—the most beautiful I had ever seen.

I forgot everything—where I was—what I was supposed to be doing. I was standing in the middle of the
stage before hundreds of people, and blocking the way
for two celebrated movie stars who had been charming
to me all day. I forgot them completely. I saw only the
girl sitting quietly at the piano below the stage, with
a slightly troubled expression in those big brown eyes,
watching me, wonderingly.

Someone shoved me, and I shuffled forward in a
daze.

All else that evening became remote, trivial, un-
real. When we left the Madison Theater and went to
other movie houses, the brown eyes seemed to follow
me.

Somehow I must have gone through all the motions
my assignment called for. Somehow the evening eventually came to a close. And somehow, after the cele-

brated stars had finished their trip around the movie houses and had gone to bed, I found myself back in the Madison Theater. Alone now, and in the last row, sitting as inconspicuously as possible in a corner, I wondered what had hit me.

Girls were a species of human beings of whom up to this moment, except for those in my own family, I was totally ignorant. My column was full of imaginary and joking references to girls who wanted to flirt with me, and girls I tried to flirt with, but actually I had never had a girl friend. Up to now my job as a newspaper reporter had been the all-absorbing passion of my life.

I listened to the girl with the brown eyes playing a piano accompaniment to the pictures that flickered across the screen. Deftly she altered the music to fit the rapidly changing scenes—crescendo for suspense, tenderness for the love scenes, a lively lilt for humor and slapstick. I wanted to move closer, where I could watch her fingers race over the keyboard, and see more than the brown hair tied back with a white ribbon that glimmered from my faraway seat in the dark. But I froze to my seat.

The picture ended. A slide appeared that said, simply and somewhat peremptorily: "GOOD NIGHT." The house lights came on.

I sat debating whether to leave or to wait while she gathered her music. The debate was settled for me. The manager came over to where I sat and stated in blunt words what I already knew.

"The show is over. The cleaning people want to get to work."

He made it plain he wanted me to clear out, and I went.

The next night I sat in the same place. Night after night I came. Invariably, I was the first to take my seat, and the last to leave. But I could only sit there and, with pounding heart and eager eyes, look and listen. I knew time was slipping. I knew someone else with more courage and resourcefulness might step in ahead of me —might already have done so.

My work suffered. My sleep at night was negligible. I lost interest in reading. I sat around the house, listless, indifferent. My thoughts were constantly on her: Who was she? Was there a boy friend? If so, could I edge him out? How could I meet her? Should I go right down and talk to her, or arrange to have someone introduce us—and, if so, who in the world could arrange that?

Mother grew concerned about my loss of appetite. Under normal conditions, I had an inordinate interest in her cooking, for even when we had very little in the house, she managed somehow to make our food appetizing. But these were not normal conditions, and I had no thought for food, or for that matter anything else, except the one great interest which now filled my heart.

Finally, after a time, I made a little progress—got up a little more courage. From the secluded corner in the last row, I slowly made my way by the tenth night to the third row in the center—right behind the orchestra pit where she sat at the piano.

That night, a small boy sat next to me, small, bespectacled, serious-minded. He sat intently watching the picture, furiously chewing gum.

"A good picture, isn't it?" I said, attempting to open a conversation with him.

"Yup," he said, without turning, and lost himself once more in the entrancing images on the screen.

I sat quietly for a while, then the resolve to do something suddenly struck me. From my vastly superior maturity, and the wide difference of perhaps six years in our ages (he looked to be about eight) I leaned over to the boy at my side and said, grandiosely, "I will give you twenty-five cents, if you will take a note down to the girl at the piano. How about it?"

He looked up at me in the semidark, and his expression was plainly saying, "If you are goofy enough to pay twenty-five cents for that, I'll do it—it's your money, but, boy, you must be nuts!"

What he did say was, "Where's the twenty-five cents, and the note?"

I quickly fished from my pocket a ragged piece of copy paper, the kind used in newspaper offices the world over, and scribbled the note. It said:

"I know it's bold to do this, but I can't think of any other way of meeting you. I would like to meet you. Would it be possible for me to see you home after the show tonight?"

The boy took the note and laid it on the piano in front of the girl's music. She came to a pause, read it, and looked around to see where it came from.

I nodded. She shook her head. And the world slipped out from under me.

My young courier, back at my side, looked at me curiously, decided his original impression was right, shrugged his shoulders—and returned to his preoccupation with the picture.

Miserable and defeated, I sat, still looking with my heart in my eyes at the girl for whom I would at that moment—and at any time all through life later—have given everything.

Before I knew it the show had ended. The familiar "GOOD NIGHT," which had become a curt intrusion upon my nightly adventure, appeared on the screen. I should have gone out then, but I didn't. The house lights came on, and there I was, trapped in the third row just behind her—bewildered and embarrassed.

She turned around, and smiled. With perhaps the greatest demand I have ever made upon my courage, I got up and made my way down to the seat nearest her. Once there, my courage and my voice left me simultaneously.

"I am sorry," I heard her say, her quiet, warm voice so singularly suited to her eyes. "I am very sorry, but my father is here to take me home tonight."

My heart became light—my hopes restored, my courage revived, my adoration multiplied.

"Could I—would you—perhaps, maybe tomorrow night?" I ventured.

"I don't know," she said. "Somebody from the family always sees me home. You could walk home with us, if you wished."

I "wished" profoundly, and said so, quickly. I would

walk with her father and mother and sister and anyone else—if only it gave me a chance of meeting her.

Tomorrow night finally came. The show was unbelievably long, but at last it ended. I waited by the piano until she arranged her music. My heart was in my mouth, and it would have gotten in the way of my words if I had had any words.

"I don't even know your name," she said. "Mine is Marion."

I told her my name, hoping that she would recognize it from the paper, but she didn't. It meant nothing to her.

I took her music and followed her up the aisle, stumbling and almost falling on the rubber matting. She noticed it, and reached out her hand to help me. I already knew she was the kind of person who would always do something like that.

She led me to her mother, who was sitting in the last row, waiting for her. When she introduced me, she added something that made my pride swell: "He seems like a very nice boy."

Marion's mother impressed me then, as she always did afterward, with her regal look and bearing, and the innate goodness which shone in her eyes and face. I felt suddenly relaxed.

I had no trouble finding things to say during the short walk to their home. The night was clear. The stars were bright. Everything about it seemed wonderful to me. We talked about the show and her music. I told her about the column I wrote for The Sunday

Charles Alden Seltzer
(1910)

Ella Albers Seltzer
(1896)

Marion Elizabeth Champlin
at the time Louis B. Seltzer
met her (1912)

Louis B. Seltzer, married man
and Police Reporter for The
Cleveland Press (1916)

A "Luee, The Offis Boy" column (1911)

Leader and she now remembered having read it. She remembered the night I had walked across the darkened stage.

"It was because I saw you that night that I thought it would be all right to see you," she said.

When we reached her home, her father was still up. He was a genial, bald-headed man, whose fringe of white hair gave him the look of "Foxy Grandpa," a beloved comic character which appeared in our paper. To make conversation I said so, and he laughed. I liked his laugh.

Like my own father, he was a carpenter by trade, and like him, he had gone through hard times. In fact, he was out of work now. Marion's income as a movie pianist was helping the family. I knew it would be another bond between us when I told her that I, too, had gone to work to help our family.

I knew I should leave, yet I couldn't, and Marion's mother finally had to send me away. But I walked up the street with my heart singing, for I would see her again the next night. I knew then, even if I was only fourteen, that this was the girl of my life; and the fact that she was the first and only girl I had ever known seemed like a blessing given me by God.

The next morning I was gay and happy. Mother watched me in surprise as I devoured my breakfast. Father was astonished at the change and said so, asking me how I explained it. I didn't. I knew they would think I was too young to fall seriously in love—and, as it turned out later, they did. For the time being, I thought it better to say nothing. I would wait until I was sure of Marion—and the mere thought of not being sure, and its implication, sent a cold chill through me.

When I went to work, Howard Denby looked at me. "What's happened to you, young man?" he asked. "We began to think you were never coming out of it."

"Out of what?" I asked.

"Out of that blue funk you've been in for the last couple of weeks," he said. "Even your writing showed it. I was intending to talk to you about it."

I put everything into the column I wrote that day, and Howard Denby complimented me on it. "Well," he said, "this is more like it."

When I finished my column, I had an irresistible impulse. I would write my first letter to Marion. I rolled another long sheet of copy paper into my typewriter and told her about myself, things that were for me easier to write than to tell. I paused only over the problem of how to address her at the beginning, and how to sign myself at the end. I decided just to write it like a letter to anyone, although it seemed cold and formal when set down that way. Then I rushed over to the Post Office, where I put a special delivery stamp on it.

That night, when I saw her, I wondered whether she had gotten it—and what she thought. "You do things in a hurry, don't you?" was her comment. But she was pleased.

A lot of copy paper was mailed to Marion after that. It was one letter a day when I saw her every night.

When I didn't, it was two or three—once as many as five!

It was a year or so later, during the big storm of 1913 which tied the whole city up as tight as a drum, that we really spent a lot of time together. By this time my parents knew Marion, and by this time I was working nights again. Marion had left school—for the same reason I had—and had a job in the music department of the May Company. At night she still played the piano, and we often had trouble finding time to meet.

The big storm of 1913 put all the power out of commission. No streetcars ran. No papers were published. Everything stopped. It was like a holiday for Marion and me, the happiest of the many happy times we have had together. It was then that we decided one day we would marry. We were only sixteen and we would have to wait; but we made up our minds.

A little less than two years later we decided we had waited long enough. Our problem was to get the consent of our parents, since their legal approval was necessary.

"You are both so young," Father protested. "Especially you, Louis. Girls sometimes marry before they are eighteen, but a boy of your age—why don't you wait?"

"We don't want to wait, Father," I said. "I have been old enough to be working for a long time now. I'm old enough to marry."

Father hesitated. He looked at Mother, and then

said, "All right, you know what you are doing, Louis. You have been out in the world much earlier than most boys, and I think you have grown up faster."

The rest of this chapter could be told, in similar words, by many hard-working young couples who were making their way in our enterprising young city in 1915. But since it happened to me, I will tell it.

The day that we were to be married, we went to work, Marion at May's and I to the paper, having arranged to meet during the lunch hour to get the license. Bill Bastian, one of the license clerks at the Court House, was a close friend, and he was nice enough to hold up his lunch hour to wait for us.

The marriage license fee was seventy-five cents. I didn't have it. After paying my streetcar fare that morning, I had only eleven cents left in my pocket. Before my embarrassment could become acute, Marion calmly reached into her pocketbook, and gave me seventy-five cents.

"I'll pay it back," I told her, as I squeezed her hand. Then I suddenly began to worry. "Do we have enough streetcar fare between us to get home?"

Marion said, "Just enough," as she happily tucked our license into her pocketbook.

When I got back to the office I called Dr. Dan F. Bradley, pastor of the Plymouth Congregational Church on West Fourteenth Street. He was one of the city's foremost ministers, and had been a good friend to me, often giving me the benefit of his wonderful philosophy. I had interviewed him many times, but this time, I explained, I was not asking for any statements. My heart warmed at his response when I asked for a quiet wedding at his home that night.

He lived only about two blocks from the movie where Marion was now playing the piano, and after the show ended we walked over there, a little nervous, and very happy. There was a bright light burning at the front of the house, and Dr. Bradley opened the door as we climbed the front steps. We sat down and talked for a few moments—until Mrs. Bradley said, "Dan, these young people didn't come here tonight to listen to you. They came to be married—remember?"

Dr. Bradley chuckled and got up. He was a tall, thin man, who looked rather like Abraham Lincoln and had the same kindly and compassionate way.

We stood by the piano in his front room. I thought it was somehow symbolic of our first meeting. I remembered the few clumsy words I first spoke to Marion, standing by the piano in the Madison Theater.

The words were more impressive now: "For better, or for worse, through sickness and in poverty, until death do you part." They burned themselves deep into my consciousness. From now on for the rest of our lives we would care for each other—make our home, have our children, make our way together.

"I know somehow that you two will be happy together," Dr. Bradley said. He smiled toward his wife. "We can usually tell, can't we, Mother?"

From the sidewalk we waved back at them as they stood in the doorway watching us. Together, arm in arm, unable to put our happiness into words, we made our way to the streetcar. On the streetcar, alone except for a man up front sound asleep, we talked and planned and hugged each other—for the first time since our marriage.

There was neither time nor money for a honeymoon for us. We stayed that night in the apartment of Marion's sister, which was in the same terrace where her parents lived, only a few doors away.

In the morning at my usual hour of six I got up and went to work. But by then it was a different job, for I have gotten ahead of my story. At the time I first met Marion, I was still writing as Luee, The Offis Boy, for the Sunday edition of The Leader. Not long afterward, I was assigned as a police reporter at $15 a week.

Chapter 9

WHEN I WAS a cub police reporter for The Leader, my boss was "Old" Bob Larkin. No drill sergeant ever cussed more colorfully than Bob Larkin, and no sergeant ever got better or quicker results. He never went to college, but he was one of the best journalism "professors" I ever knew.

Old Bob was a cantankerous, scowling, pipe-smoking, spirit-breaking taskmaster. He redeemed himself by doing more than he asked of others and working, if anything, twice as hard as anybody else. He made the entire West Side my "beat." I was held responsible for everything that happened, as he put it, "west of the river"—the river being the Cuyahoga, whose winding channel splits Greater Cleveland almost in the very center. I had to cover five police stations and an equal number of fire headquarters, and anything I missed was directly my responsibility.

It was Old Bob's idea that we should walk the "beat," which for me, in the course of a single night, represented about fifteen miles. This had to be done between eight P.M. when I came on duty and four A.M. when the morning deadline made useless any further coverage. Old Bob insisted that we also stop at drugstores, confectionery shops, saloons, and other places between police and fire stations.

"Do that every night and you get to know everybody on the West Side, what they're doing and what they're thinking, and you develop a lot of news sources," he said, in giving me my original instructions.

"And I want you to call me frequently during the night. I want to know where you are, and how fast I can get to you. I'll have all the telephone numbers right here." He pointed to a beat-up index box he kept at hand on a ledge.

At first, I rebelled inwardly at working for Old Bob. He was curt, even rude and cutting, in his remarks when we failed to get all the facts on a given story.

"That the best you can do?" he snarled. "How about these questions?"

In rapid-fire order he would ask a dozen questions which I had overlooked.

"Get back, and get the answers," he ordered.

He also demanded politeness from his young reporters.

"Yes, sir," I replied, very politely.

I went back, and got the information he wanted. "That will teach you for the next time," he said. "Get it the first time, and you won't have to go back."

After a while I got to know just what Old Bob wanted —he wanted everything. Just when you thought you had everything, he thought of something else. He never seemed satisfied.

But his method worked. The fear of his disapproval was far stronger than any inclination to take the easy way out.

Old Bob was the fiercest competitor I ever knew in our business, and, when eventually one got to know him, the most lovable character. He never spoke to reporters for other papers. He ignored them entirely.

His paper came first, and there wasn't even a close second to it. He lived and breathed for the paper. Anybody who let it down was worse in Old Bob's book than Benedict Arnold ever dared to be.

For a large part of each evening Old Bob would be on the telephone, calling the "rounds." This was the process of meticulously telephoning every standard news source both in the city and around its principal suburbs. It was a tedious task, but Old Bob insisted upon keeping up this nightly telephone contact himself.

This was done from his "office" on the second floor of the antiquated Champlain Avenue Police Headquarters—an absurdly small and dark cubicle which once had been an old elevator shaft. His equipment consisted of a single chair without a back, three telephones, and a whole array of boxes in which were phone numbers, clippings, and assorted information that he considered indispensable to his job as Chief Police Reporter for The Leader.

Woe betide a competitor's reporter if he dared loiter within hearing distance of Old Bob. There was a drinking fountain about twenty feet from his elevator-shaft office, the only place on the whole floor where a drink of water could be obtained. But let an opposition reporter bend over for an extra minute to take on a refreshing supply of water, and Old Bob was out of his office, telephone dangling at his "desk," chasing the opposition reporter belligerently. If the competitor didn't take off fast enough, he was helped along in whatever way hands or feet deemed most appropriate.

"Get out of here, and stay out of here," Old Bob would shout.

Among newspaper reporters a practice called "syndicating" was then common—and today, regrettably, still exists. It is simply the pooling of information among reporters from different papers to render their respective jobs that much easier, and to protect one another against getting "scooped."

Old Bob was instant death on anyone he caught "syndicating." The guilty reporter was fired on the spot. To trip up a reporter under him (or on some other paper) who was suspected of "syndicating" or of benefiting from the unworthy practice, he set up elaborate plans for detection.

On one occasion in particular he put into an unsealed

envelope a story about a shooting scrape, complete with names, addresses, occupations, police officers' names, and all the essential facts for a comprehensive story. The story was a complete fake, and Old Bob arranged with his own office that it was to be ignored completely when it came in.

The young reporter who was charged with getting the unsealed envelope to The Leader office—an errand he performed several times each night—somehow was "intercepted" by an opposition representative. The next morning the story appeared in the opposition newspaper, much to Old Bob's gratification, and not, of course, in his own paper, The Leader. He fired the young reporter and, outlining the exact detail of his plot, warned that anybody who made the same mistake would receive the same medicine.

Old Bob likewise was fastidious about facts. He never tolerated a misstatement, an inaccuracy in name or address or any other essential of a story.

"It's up to us to get it right, and by God we're going to get it right, no matter what we have to do to accomplish it," he would say, over and over again.

No young reporter could have had a more severe or more difficult superior for whom to work. By the same token no young reporter could have had a more graphic lesson in the underlying thoroughness and integrity of his business.

I am not alone in expressing the belief that Old Bob Larkin was the best teacher of journalism—practical journalism—that the Middle West ever had. There are, all through American journalism today—from New York to San Francisco, from the Great Lakes to the Gulf—men in key positions on newspapers whose dedication to their profession came from the example set by the rugged old police reporter, Bob Larkin.

His steel-rimmed spectacles were always dirty even though he never appeared to take them off, or rub his stubby fingers across them. He kept his evil-smelling pipe in his mouth constantly, and when he talked he sprayed his words at anybody within a few feet. He never saw much that was funny about life, but sympathized quickly under his frigid facade with those who were genuinely in trouble or suddenly confronted with tragedy.

He had an uncanny ability to distinguish the legitimate from the phony, and was impatient with those who tried to soft-soap him, whether in his own business or outside. There wasn't a cop or a fireman who didn't swear by Old Bob Larkin even at the very moment he might be swearing at him.

In many respects he was an eccentric. A beat-up motorcycle was his only means of travel. He wouldn't ride in a streetcar, and certainly not in an automobile. He was penurious about the company's money, and prudent about his own. He never told a lie that any man who ever worked with him or for him detected. We all thought he was utterly incapable of untruth or dishonesty.

Several years later, when I was working for The Cleveland Press, and assumed some executive responsibility, the first thing I did was to prevail upon the Editor to hire Old Bob Larkin.

"Why, he's an old man," the Editor said. "He wouldn't work out for us. He's almost through."

I urged strongly nevertheless that we hire him, pointing out that nobody in our business knew as much about Cleveland, its police and fire business, its personalities, its skeletons, its backgrounds, as Bob Larkin —and that there wasn't a better journalism teacher anywhere. Finally, I got my way.

Old Bob never permitted that fact to color his attitude. He regarded me as impersonally as he did every boss for whom he worked. It was the paper—the business—the sacred process of searching out the cold abstract facts with which to illuminate the day's record that mattered exclusively to Bob Larkin.

In every city in America there probably has been some newspaper personality like Old Bob. He may not always be Chief Police Reporter. He might even be an editor. But, behind the headlines, behind the stories that appear in a newspaper, in cities both large and small, there is somewhere a man dedicated to the principle that the truth is the ultimate mission of a newspaperman's life, that, above and beyond all else. Nowadays, in many places, there may even be a feminine counterpart of Old Bob, although, when his image comes into the mind's eye, that is rather hard to imagine.

When Bob Larkin, in one of his rare moments, put his hand on my shoulder and said, "Son, you never let me down—that is, knowingly"—that was praise from Caesar. I never forgot it, or the man to whom many of us are so much indebted for what we have done, in the profession he loved with the belligerence of an old Bengal tiger.

Chapter 10

WHEN I WAS fifteen I was fired from The Leader. It was the hardest blow I had ever received.

Sam Anson, the City Editor, called me in.

"I don't like to say this to you, Louie," Mr. Anson said, "but we have to let you go. You are just not cut out for the newspaper business. You are young and you should look for some other kind of job. You could walk through news knee deep in rubber boots and not see it, even if it was all around you. You don't have the nose for it. I used to think you did, and Chester Hope thought so, but we're convinced you don't. I am sorry, Louie, but that's it."

I turned my badge, No. 26, over to Mr. Anson, with a numb sensation. I couldn't reconcile this decision with the fact that for so long a time I had faithfully written the Luee, The Offis Boy column, had covered other assignments as well, and had handled to the best of my ability a police reporter's job. Somewhere I had fallen down on the job, and I didn't even know where.

I had always liked Sam Anson and I didn't feel bitter toward him now. He had taken away my first job, but he was the one who had given it to me.

He was one of the greatest newspapermen I have ever known, a man of extraordinary gifts, and a great and legendary figure in our business. He used to send a man clear out to the periphery of the town as soon as a report of fire or disaster or murder came in, not waiting until the exact location was discovered.

"Get out there, and then call me," he would say.

By this tactic he invariably had a time-beat of minutes on the opposition.

I am sure Sam Anson was honest when he told me that he thought I would do better in some other field, but his words had exactly the opposite effect. I was determined to prove him wrong. I made up my mind that I would be a newspaperman—or I would break myself in the process. I would show them. I would go to another newspaper and get a job.

I tried The Press first, only to be told they were filled up. I tried the other papers, and there were no jobs there, either. Then I began to look elsewhere. I had to get a job. Father was doing well now, and it was no longer a question of helping the family. It was altogether a question of myself. My pride was badly hurt and I had to get a job. I began to look everywhere.

I went to the House of Hubbell on a downtown street in Cleveland. This was an advertising agency which also published house organs for industrial firms and stores.

"If you can write, I have a job for you," said O. S. Hubbell, the head of the company. "We need someone to write small items for a couple of house organs—someone who can write advertising also."

I took the job, at $6 a week. The hours were regular, which was something new in my experience. On a newspaper, the hours were long and irregular, stretching sometimes to sixteen or eighteen a day if a big story was breaking.

Everything was different here. The office was quiet and orderly. People talked in low voices. There was no hurry, no litter around the desks, no smell of ink and paper. After several years of working against the roar of the presses, I felt as if I were surrounded by the unearthly quiet of a cemetery.

For over a year I worked faithfully for the House of Hubbell. Everything I was asked to do I did, but my heart was not in my work.

One day I went to my boss. "I am sorry, Mr. Hubbell," I said. "You have been good to me here, but I am in the wrong place. I have to try to get a job on a newspaper. That's the only place I'll be happy." I left the House of Hubbell with no job, and not knowing whether I could get one.

I had always thought The Cleveland Press was the best paper in town—ever since at the age of eight I had delivered its home edition from porch to porch in our West Side neighborhood. That was where I had always

wanted to work. So once again I went to the office of
The Press.

The Editor's office was in a cupola on top of the
building, reached by a circular iron stairway. I climbed
up. Victor Morgan, the Editor, sat behind a huge desk.
He was a big, blond man with a stern face—a powerful
and positive man. He wasted no words.

"What is it?" he asked.

"I would like a job, Mr. Morgan," I said. Before he
could answer, I went on. "I'll make a bargain with you,
Mr. Morgan. Let me go out on my own for a week, and
write for The Press each day. I will get my own stories,
write them, and turn them in to you. I want more than
anything in the world to be on The Press. I have always
wanted to be here. I would appreciate it very much if
you gave me this chance."

Victor Morgan had listened. He looked sharply at
me. I was seventeen, and I suppose I looked younger.

"All right," he said, "it's a bargain. It's your risk.
You asked for it. Now it's up to you to deliver."

Never did I work so hard. Never did I walk so much
or to so many places. Each day I came back to The Press
office, sat at a typewriter, and wrote out my stories.

My hope began to rise on the second day when the
paper rolled off the presses and I saw one of my stories,
printed just as I had written it. Others were printed.
Before the week was up, Victor Morgan stopped at the
desk where I was pounding away with my index fingers
at a typewriter and said, "Come to work, tomorrow.
You've got a job."

I almost let out an Indian war whoop the way my

mother had years before when Father sold his first short story. For me the event was equally significant. I was back in my beloved newspaper business, with the paper I'd always wanted to be on, and I intended to stay there —all of my life.

Chapter 11

I WAS ASSIGNED to Police Headquarters during my first year at The Press. I saw much there, as I now know, that shaped my attitudes for the future. I began to realize what I would like to do, if given the opportunity, to help improve and strengthen the processes of law and administration.

At "Police" I reported to George Tratzmiller. He and my old friend, Bob Larkin of The Leader, were mortal journalistic enemies, ceaselessly engaged, not only in a newspaper fight, but in a personal vendetta. They were both good, they both worked hard, and I learned a lot by watching both of them. Hours were nothing to me. Assignments I took in stride, no matter where they were, or how rough. Always I reached out for more to do. I was not going to be set back again if hard work could prevent it.

The Police Court was then still in an antiquated building above a stable on the long-since obliterated Champlain Avenue. On a hot day the court smelled. It was hard to know whether it smelled from the stables below—or the corruption within the courtroom.

I saw there raw, grim, slick, ruthless, debauching influences at work—influences to circumvent justice, to pollute and corrupt at the very source of law enforcement.

"Louie," a big, tall lawyer said to me one day, "I would like to talk to you." He took me aside, lowering his voice as he continued, "You get the information on cases, tell me which policemen are working on what matters, and act as my ears and eyes—and I will see to it that you make more money than your paper pays you."

He was rich. He owned a huge house, where he wined and dined many people. There were reporters, I knew, who were more than good friends, and the Police Chief visited his house regularly. Judges stopped there likewise.

I wasn't interested in his offer. When I told George Tratzmiller about it, he said, "I expected it. He has made himself a power around here. He gets most of the business. He pays off most of the people."

"Why doesn't someone do something about it?" I asked.

"Nobody will talk," George explained. "Too many are in on it."

Gradually I learned about a number of such sub-surface arrangements which, at the time, prevailed

around Police Court and Police Headquarters. Slowly
my anger was aroused. With George Tratzmiller's per-
mission, I talked with the Editor, Victor Morgan, and
told him what I had seen.

"It's bad," said Morgan. "It's getting worse. Somehow
we've got to find a way to break it up."

He sent men to Police Headquarters, ostensibly on
other assignments. They worked carefully and unob-
trusively. They checked records and cases. The more we
unearthed the surer we were that the stench came from
the Police Court rather than from the stables. And yet,
after months of effort, we were no nearer to breaking
it up than when we started. The covering of tracks was
accomplished effectively. No one would talk, and no
break could come without someone talking.

I watched and studied and talked to people, learn-
ing from George Tratzmiller, and others, all it was
possible to know about the techniques, the methods,
the nature of the chain forged by the manipulators of
Police Court and Police Headquarters.

I also learned that the majority of policemen, the
majority of judges and court attachés, were honest and
honorable—but helpless against the intricate and tight
machine that time and trickery had created.

The time came when I was transferred. The Press
was waging a fierce campaign against Harry L. Davis,
who was three times Mayor of Cleveland, later to be
Governor of Ohio, and considered politically impreg-
nable. In the heat of this campaign I was assigned to
cover City Hall.

The Press was poison ivy at City Hall, and all doors were shut against Press reporters. It was my job, nonetheless, to "cover" it. I was not responsible for the paper's policy. I was responsible for getting news out of City Hall.

On my first day on the job I was instructed by my City Desk to ask the Mayor certain questions. I stepped into his reception room. Big Nate Cook, the Mayor's secretary, saw me, and he knew I was from The Press.

"See that line," he said, belligerently, pointing to the floor where a doorway separated the outer reception room, where I stood, and the Mayor's office, in which he stood.

"That line says no reporter for The Press crosses it," he said. "If they do they'll get thrown out on their rump; and I am the fellow who will do it."

I looked at Nate Cook, and I decided he meant it, but I was a reporter for The Press. I had a job to do, and I was going to do it. I walked toward him.

"I'm going to see the Mayor, Nate, and I don't want any trouble," I said.

"Cross that line, and you'll get trouble," Cook threatened.

"Nate, I am here for a story," I said. "I'm going to get it. You may get me a better one. The better one will be if you do throw me out. I'm coming in, Nate. It's up to you."

I started coming. I kept right on. Within a step of Nate Cook I saw him clench his fists. I thought that would probably be the end of me, but I kept walking.

Nate stepped aside.

"You little—" he said. But I saw the Mayor.

Nate Cook became my good friend eventually. No matter how hard The Press fought against Davis, it was always possible after that for a Press reporter to cross, unharmed and unchallenged, the line Nate Cook had one day drawn there.

The story got around, and helped me in other circles as well. And I had learned a lesson from the incident: When a newspaperman has a job to do, and does it, he is respected for it.

City Hall was my beat for a year, during the most vicious battle between a city administration and a newspaper Cleveland had ever seen—up to that time. At the end of the year I was called into The Press office. I went on general assignment—an assignment which presumes that a reporter associated with a newspaper in that capacity is automatically endowed with an infinite variety of skills.

One morning in 1915, I had to tear myself away from home to go to work, and for a very good reason. My son had been born the night before.

Mr. Morgan shook my hand and said, very seriously, "Good morning, Father." I was embarrassed when he added, "Where are the cigars?"

The truth was I couldn't afford to buy any. He knew that.

We couldn't afford the hospital, either, and our son was born at home, in part of a two-family house on West Boulevard, where we lived with Marion's parents. We had no car or telephone, and in the middle of the night

I had run down Madison Avenue to fetch Dr. Hartzell, running faster even than the night I had fetched Dr. Medlin for Father—and feeling just as terrified.

Mr. Morgan pulled a box of cigars out from behind his back and handed it to me.

"This is on condition that you tell me what this new young man's name is," the Editor stipulated.

I hesitated. "Maybe you won't like this, Mr. Morgan," I said, "but we named him after another editor."

"You still haven't told me his name."

"It's Chester—after Mr. Chester Hope, who was Sunday Editor of The Leader," I said. "He was my special friend when I needed one most."

Mr. Morgan said, "A good name, for a good man."

My desk was now up front near Mr. Morgan's office. Each day, in addition to my general assignments, I was writing editorials. They began to appear regularly on the editorial page, some of them signed by Mr. Morgan. I felt that I was making steady progress.

It wasn't long before I began to feel I had made too much progress.

When Chester, our son, was three months old, Mr. Morgan called me in, and said he was appointing me City Editor of The Press, effective the following day. I couldn't believe him.

"What's the matter, Louie?" he asked. "Don't you want the job?"

"I do, Mr. Morgan," I said. "But I am surprised. I didn't dream it would happen."

Naturally I had thought about some day being City Editor—but not so soon. At little more than nineteen,

I was six years out of grade school—married—had a son —and was now City Editor of the paper for which I had the greatest love. Things had happened fast.

The next morning I reported to work in a state of almost complete shock. In general I knew what the job was. I had watched it operate as a reporter taking assignments from the City Editor. Beyond that, I knew only that it was one of the toughest jobs on any newspaper. To make matters even worse, the City Editor whose place I was taking had already left, so there was no one around to "break me in."

Well, I thought, I had a job to do. I had better get at it.

It *was* tough. I got down to the paper early and I stayed late. I had never worked as hard before at any job. Fortunately for me, the whole staff worked with me, and we had some tremendous stories. But the fact remained that I still looked a lot like the "Luee" of my first column. People visiting the office sometimes mistook me for one of the office boys, and two of them, actually, were older than I.

An elderly man one day stopped at the City Desk and asked to talk to the City Editor. When I explained that I *was* the City Editor he insisted on seeing the Editor and demanded acidly of Mr. Morgan, "Are you running a kindergarten out there?"

My trouble was not only that I looked young—I *was* young, and I lacked experience. Situations were too intricate for me, too complicated in many instances. This worried me, and the more I worried, the harder I worked.

Strangely enough, Mr. Morgan, with a City Editor who had no formal education, tended to hire reporters who had been to college. Practically every new man came direct from a university, and while they were generally very cooperative, this added to my anxiety. They were older than I, and they knew more than I.

I received a substantial increase in pay after three months, and Mr. Morgan complimented me on the job I was doing. But I knew I was not really qualified by experience or maturity, or knowledge—either of our own business or of the many complicated kinds of information we had to deal with—to handle the job as it should be handled.

I had to force the issue. I went to Mr. Morgan and asked to be relieved of the City Editorship, quickly adding, "I would like to tell you why."

I stated my doubts and misgivings frankly, and told him that it would be better, I believed, for both the paper and myself if I were returned to the staff in some reportorial capacity—until I was more adequately seasoned with the required experience.

He thought I was making a mistake, but he agreed.

"I never heard of anybody firing himself from a job like this before," he said. "I have to admire you for it. What about becoming Political Editor of the paper?"

This was the field in which I had been most interested ever since I started to work, and a week later I made the change. Mr. Morgan saw to it that I also wrote at least two editorials a day; most of the time I initiated the subjects for them, and many of them began to appear on Page One.

It was up to me now to equip myself for any future responsibility that might come my way. I knew my decision had jeopardized my chance for a future executive job on the paper, that the chance might not come again. I was sure, however, that for the paper, as well as for myself, I had done the right thing. The future would take care of itself, if I worked hard.

Chapter 12

ON JULY 4, 1919, it looked as if all of America had converged upon Toledo, Ohio. That was the occasion, as sports fans no doubt remember, of the classic battle between Jess Willard and Jack Dempsey for the heavyweight championship of the world. There wasn't a hotel room to be had for any price in the whole town. Everything had been solidly booked for months in advance.

For days people had been sleeping on benches, on blankets in the parks, on porches all around the town. Many of them had to walk miles to lay their heads on a porch swing or a hammock. It was not unusual to see a fastidiously dressed gentleman—complete with traditional diamond stickpin, stiff cuffs, and shimmering cravat, even in the broiling heat of July—reclining on somebody's porch, for a price, to catch his night's sleep.

Transportation of any kind was at a premium, if not unobtainable. Hotel lobbies were impossible to get into, and, once in, it almost cost your life, and certainly bruises and shin-cracking, to get out again. For color, for excitement, for tension, for wide-open betting with odds fluctuating wildly, for confusion and chaos, nothing else I have ever seen even remotely equaled that event.

The lean, trim, hard-looking, then flat-nosed Jack Dempsey was at once surrounded by great throngs whenever he appeared anywhere. He couldn't even move more than a few steps. The same was true of big, genial, towering Jess Willard, who appeared singularly shy for a man so widely acclaimed as a world champion.

The facilities for covering such a great story in 1919 were vastly different from those of today. Television did not exist. Radio was not yet practicable. The "broadcast" was just beginning, and the few sets in use were mostly of the "oatmeal box" kind—so called because they were made with the tuning coil wound around the outside of oatmeal boxes picked off pantry shelves. Movies were being taken, but they would not be exhibited until days later. The immediate coverage of the fight on that July 4, 1919, was strictly up to the newspapers.

Almost the whole staff of The Cleveland Press, far smaller in 1919 than it is today, was called into action —either at the office, handling the fight as it came through, or on the scene at the vast, improvised Bay View Park Arena in Toledo where the great sports

event was taking place. It was our job to make sure that
our paper would be out first and out in front in dispatches, in color stories, and in pictures. The stories
could be telephoned or wired, but getting the pictures
back in those days took careful, intricate planning.

At that time we had three photographers. All were
sent to Toledo to take pictures of the fight. With them
were sent three reporters assigned to act as couriers
for bringing the plates straight from the camera back
to Cleveland by plane or automobile.

The first pictures into Cleveland from the fight had
a financial as well as a news value. The paper that got
them out first was bound to see many thousands of
extras.

It would take several hours, no matter how fast we
worked, to get the pictures in from Toledo, process
them, and get them into the "Fight Extra."

Arrangements of an infinite variety had to be made,
for transportation, for the housing of photographers
and reporters, and, far more important than all else,
for the seats at the fight itself. I was to go to Toledo
several days in advance to make these arrangements on
the scene for our staff.

We went out to sprawling Bay View Park Arena three
days before the fight to spot our locations and to "case"
the place so that every step and every minute of time
could be planned. Time was the most important element with which we were confronted. We arranged
that one photographer was to take from his particular
position the action in the first round. He was instantly
to give his plates to the reporter who would be sitting

right at his elbow, and that reporter was to make a dash —his exit was also carefully expedited—to either car or plane. The other two photographers were to cover the second and third rounds in the same way. All three photographers were then to stay at the scene for the full fight, so that on the following day The Press would have complete pictorial coverage.

We were among the hundreds who had no rooms. One of our reporters had friends living in Toledo who graciously turned over their front porch to us. It was a stifling night, and with no pillows, and nothing whatever to ease the hard floor of the porch, sleeping was out of the question.

The day of the fight was one of the hottest days of that summer. The event was scheduled for afternoon, but before daybreak people started for the Bay View Park Arena. They paid whatever the asking price might be for whatever food was available. Many, like us, had had no sleep. Most walked to the scene of the fight.

The place was literally packed, but luckily our seats were well toward the ring. They had to be. Cameras in 1919 were not the amazingly effective instruments, equipped with powerful telescopic lenses, that they are today. They were cumbersome, box-like affairs, much harder to handle.

My seat was an enviable one, close to the Dempsey side of the ring, but I was not there to watch the great fighter in action. I was located where I could see, signal to the photographers, and check on the exit of the couriers. The fight for us was incidental. Our obliga-

Four generations of Seltzers—
Charles Alden, Lucien Bonaparte, Louis Benson, and Chester Ellsworth (1919)

The John W. Davis scoop (1924)

Louis B. Seltzer, newly
appointed Editor of The
Cleveland Press (1928)

Newton D. Baker *(standing left)* defends Louis B. Seltzer
(seated far right) (1929)

tion was to get the pictures and put them on their way as fast as was humanly possible to Cleveland.

The fight began. Our pictures of the first round were taken. The plates were handed to the first courier, and he went on his way. I watched to make sure he got out of the fight arena. The second round came up, and the process was repeated.

In the third round Dempsey came out of his corner like a ferocious animal, and battered the big Willard all over the ring. It didn't seem possible for the fight to last very long, and we had to be prepared for that, also. I directed the third courier, who was originally supposed to take off immediately with pictures of the third round, to stay until the fight was over—until the knockout picture, which would be the most important picture of all, was taken.

I sent the courier to the nearest exit—ready to race to his car as soon as the plate was handed to him—and I took his place at the side of our photographer.

The third round was over. The bell rang for the fourth round. Willard, bloody, battered, and beaten, did not come out. The fight was over. The photographer shot a picture of the referee holding up Dempsey's right hand, handed the plate to me, and I raced to the courier at the exit—getting knocked down twice on my way to him. Away he went.

My part in the great event was over, but it would be some hours before I knew the results back in Cleveland. It was impossible to call the office. Telephones and telegraph wires were pre-empted by the prior claims of sports writers telling the dramatic story to their news-paper offices all over the country. Together the last photographer—Louis Van Oeyen—and I made our way to Cleveland by train, the only means of transportation left since our cars and planes had been used by the couriers.

For several hours, as the train moved at what we thought was a snail's pace, we didn't know what had happened back home—whether the carefully worked-out plans of many weeks, and the hectic action of that afternoon, had given the paper a great picture scoop, or whether, by some unexpected turn, we had been beaten.

When we got off the train at Cleveland we saw our "Fight Extra"—and there were the pictures displayed all over Page One. That was pleasant reassurance. The pictures had come through, and they were good. But the big question remained unanswered. We raced up the street from the railway depot.

Nobody had to tell us that The Press had scored a "beat." Every face in the office, though tired and per-spiring, was beaming—an eloquent enough answer to our anxious question.

We were happy that night at The Cleveland Press—that July 4, 1919. The Dempsey-Willard fight was an unforgettable sports spectacle for the thousands who were fortunate enough to jam Bay View Park Arena that afternoon. It was perhaps even more unforgettable for the newsmen who prepared so meticulously to over-come the many obstacles which no longer—in this technoscientific age of newspaper pictures—are faced in our business.

Looking back upon it there is no doubt that we overstaffed, overarranged, overspent to set up every precaution and make sure we'd come through with the big scoop. But we did it, and that was what counted. We couldn't afford to do otherwise. And today, although the circumstances are altogether different, the same spirit prevails at The Cleveland Press, and at all other newspaper offices all over America. You do what you have to do in the time and under the circumstances where, and when, it is called for. The newspaper business has from the beginning been one in which enterprise, initiative, ingenuity, resourcefulness, and audacity have been combined to produce results. It requires these today—even more, if anything, in competition with science's modern instantaneous communications —than ever before.

There is only one Dempsey-Willard fight in a lifetime, and it happened in the times when sweat, effort, initiative, and hurdling of tough obstacles made the big scoop a tremendous newspaper exploit. There were other big "Special Extras" after the Dempsey-Willard fight, but not many and surely none so dramatic. Eventually, the great newspaper extra yielded to radio's ability to reach people faster with the flash news upon which the extra had been based. The public scarcely realized it when the extra faded from the American scene. There were no obsequies, no ceremonies, no regrets. But there is still nostalgia in the hearts of newspapermen who taxed their ingenuity to the utmost to rush the news into print—and who felt perhaps the greatest thrill of their lifetime when the cry of "Extra, Extra" rose on the streets and they knew they had scored a beat.

Chapter 13

ONE DAY IN MAY of 1920, I went down to Police Court to talk with the Chief Justice of the Municipal Court, William H. McGannon, a generally popular and respected jurist whom I liked personally very much. He had attracted notice by introducing a number of court reforms and was being talked of as a candidate for Mayor.

He greeted me with a deep, pleasant voice and the charming manner he displayed toward everyone. He was an imposing and distinguished-looking man, and I reflected that he would make a powerful candidate. It was generally agreed that if he got, and accepted, the nomination, he was almost certain of election.

During the interview he indicated some interest in the candidacy, and I went back to The Press and wrote a story on it.

That very night, an automobile salesman, Harold C. Kagy, was shot and killed in one of Cleveland's least desirable downtown neighborhoods. It later developed that Chief Justice McGannon, in company with a notorious saloon-keeper, Johnny Joyce, and the slain man, Harold Kagy, had driven together to the spot where Kagy was found dead of bullet wounds. When the police arrived, both McGannon and Joyce were gone, but McGannon's automobile was found at the scene of the murder.

Late that night, the Chief Justice called me at my home, his voice almost unrecognizable from emotion and strain. He asked me if I would hurry out to see him, and I went immediately.

Mrs. McGannon, her eyes noticeably red, let me in and took me to him. Then she left us.

"Louie, what do I do?" The Chief Justice was now a disheveled man, his eyes swollen, his mind ragged. He was obviously overcome by fear.

"What do I do?" he kept repeating over and over. I sat down to try to analyze the situation.

"First, Judge, what did happen?" I asked. "Did you kill Kagy?"

"No, no, no," he shouted hoarsely, trying to keep his voice down so that Mrs. McGannon would not hear him.

"If you didn't kill Kagy, then isn't it a simple question of telling the truth?" I asked.

"I can't," he said, "I can't."

"If you don't, you will get yourself in all kinds of trouble," I pointed out. "You of all persons should know that. If you admit that you were with Joyce and

Kagy—no matter why—and tell exactly what happened —it will turn out all right."

"But I can't," he again repeated. "If I say that I was with them, I'm through."

He wouldn't listen. His mind was so stunned that he probably didn't even hear me. Vainly, I tried to persuade him that his obvious course was both logical and simple: he should tell the truth even if it was so embarrassing to him that it might cost him his place on the Bench, and surely any chance of being nominated to the Mayor's office.

"I just wanted you to come out to talk to me, Louie," he said. "I know that you will respect my confidence. But I can't do anything else. I just have to hope."

He didn't elaborate on this. He sat, a frightened, broken, confused man, in sharp contrast to the magnificently calm and judicial Chief Justice with whom, only that day, I had talked so confidently about his chances for being Mayor of Cleveland.

"If I can do anything for you, Judge, I'll be only too glad," I said, leaving his house, as he stood in the doorway in a rumpled bathrobe, his unshaved face and swollen eyes making him a more tragic figure than any I had ever seen. "I only wish, though, that you would do for yourself what you would expect somebody else to do under these circumstances."

I was not to see Judge McGannon again for some weeks. Joyce was tried for murder and acquitted. In his trial McGannon's connection with the whole story came out, because those who were interested in Joyce's ultimate acquittal naturally brought it out.

It was my assignment both to cover the Joyce trial and to follow through any subsequent developments. The "subsequent developments" were not long in coming. The Grand Jury was called to consider Chief Justice McGannon's part in the Kagy murder, since Joyce had been legally exonerated.

The jury met on the fifth floor of an antiquated building on the Public Square. Its elevators were of the old "lift" type, pulled by cable, and open all around. It took an eternity to get from the ground floor to the fifth.

Eddie Stanton was the Prosecutor. Only he and his assistants were permitted in the Jury Room; reporters were kept waiting in an anteroom throughout the deliberations. Excitement was high. Everybody who went in or out of the Jury Room was instantly approached with a barrage of questions from the newsmen.

It was eleven o'clock of the second day of the trial. Prosecutor Stanton came out of the Jury Room. He was quickly surrounded.

"Nothing yet," he said. "I'll be back in a minute."

Stanton went to the elevator, and we all returned to our waiting places. A sudden hunch struck me. Quietly I slipped out of the room. Instead of going down by elevator, I ran down the five flights of stairs and was at the bottom when Stanton landed by elevator.

"Mind if I walk with you, Eddie?" I asked.

The Prosecutor said nothing. I interpreted that to mean that he had no objection, so I fell into step alongside him, also saying nothing. He went over to an adjoining building, up a flight of steps, and into the Law Library. He picked out a heavy volume, sat down and looked through it. When he found what he wanted, he took a piece of foolscap from a table and placed it in the spot he had found.

Without a word, he started back to the building where the Jury was deliberating. We got into the elevator together. He opened the book, turned so that I could read it, and looked up at me. As I scanned the page, his finger went to a paragraph entitled "Second Degree Murder." I studied his face anxiously, and his eyes looked steadily back into mine.

"Is that it?" I murmured.

He said nothing, but his finger came down hard on the words "Second Degree."

"Thanks," I said softly.

I didn't get off the elevator. I went back with it on its interminable trip downstairs and rushed to a telephone.

"Judge McGannon indicted for second degree murder," I told the City Desk.

The phone at the other end of the line was slammed down. Nobody even took the time to answer me. I went back upstairs.

In a half hour all creation broke loose. Phones buzzed. Reporters scurried. Doors were pounded. The Press had an extra on the street with a bannerline saying that McGannon had been indicted for second degree murder.

The reporters all shouted at once as Prosecutor Stanton poked his head out of the room.

"I can't say anything to anyone while this Jury is deliberating," he said.

"Can't you even tell us whether it's true?" someone shouted.

The Jury Foreman was at the Prosecutor's elbow. The door went shut.

The reporters streamed to the Judge's office. No indictment had been returned to him, he asserted; and until it was, it was not of record.

I was called to the phone. The Editor was on the line.

"What about this story denying McGannon's indictment?" he shouted at me.

"McGannon has been indicted," I said. Without amplifying my statement, I stood by my interpretation of what had gone on between the Prosecutor and myself.

"You've lost your job, if he hasn't been," my Editor shouted back at me.

In ten minutes the Prosecutor and the Jury Foreman came out, walked to the Judge's office, and handed him a document. The Judge then turned to us.

"Here, gentlemen, is the Jury's action in the McGannon case," he said. "The indictment is for second degree murder."

In my relief I almost keeled over. The one against whom I leaned was the County Prosecutor who, without ever saying a word, had given me the most unorthodox—and the most precarious—scoop of my whole newspaper career.

If I had been Editor of the paper at the time, I would have fired the reporter who put over this particular scoop. But fortunately that Editor didn't. He increased

the reporter's salary $10 a week, and delivered a stern
lecture, warning him never again to take such a chance.
The reporter heeded his Editor's counsel—up to a point.

The ten-dollar raise I got the day McGannon was
indicted doesn't sound very impressive nowadays, but
it was important to our little family. Our daughter had
been born in 1919, and now we were living in a crowded
house with Marion's parents and her brother-in-law
and sister. The rent had been increased twice. Marion's
father had no work, and her brother-in-law's job paid
very little. What we managed to pool together barely
made ends meet.

Marion had handled all our money since the day we
married, and she managed well. I didn't realize how
well until one night when we sat down to talk about
what we would do.

"I talked with a man today who is building some
houses up the street right above the New York Central
tracks," she said. "Now that you've got a raise, we can
take our $300 in Liberty Bonds and make a down pay-
ment on our own house. We wouldn't always be paying
rent to somebody else. We would have something to
show for it."

This represented a staggering obligation, the biggest
by far we had considered assuming. We were then
twenty-three.

"What about your parents?" I asked.

"We could build a double family place, upstairs and
down, and they could live up," Marion said.

We made up our minds to do it.

The house was only half up when, in 1921, the Editor once more offered me the City Editorship of The Press. I took it eagerly. The almost four years since I had it before had given me enough experience and knowledge about our business to convince me that this time I would stay with it.

Chapter 14

ONE BIG SITUATION after another developed in Cleveland and Ohio politics in the twenties. The showdown came on control of Ohio politics—in Cincinnati, in Columbus, and in Cleveland. The big-city bosses were putting up a struggle to fend off what eventually turned out to be an inevitable tide against them. But while I was writing politics for The Cleveland Press and handling the City Desk, they were fighting—and fighting spectacularly. The Press was fighting against them with all its power and resources, and that put me in the very center of it.

I was getting an education in the practical processes of American politics and government, an education unobtainable anywhere else. The "professors" were the politicians who sought to debauch it. The education included how votes were bought, how elections were rigged, how political machines operated from way back behind the scenes, how men got rich from this brand of politics—how taxpayers footed the bill, and how good men and women were thwarted in their efforts to gain public office. It was a liberal education.

Maurice Maschke was one of the country's top big-city political bosses. Erudite and Harvard-educated, he was a successful lawyer, a shrewd political strategist and manipulator, a man of personal charm, and politically the most potent force in Ohio politics. He made and broke public officials almost at will. Personally, I liked him. Professionally, I stood squarely with our paper. I abhorred all that he stood for in "profit politics"—the politics for which tribute was exacted, from which men grew rich and powerful beyond the influence government intended they should ever possess.

He didn't always win. Sometimes he lost big, the way he won big. One such instance was in 1921 when Fred Kohler, formerly Chief of Police, ran for Mayor.

Kohler, whom Theodore Roosevelt once described as the best Police Chief in the country, had been kicked out of office when he was caught, shoes in hand, coming out of the back door of his mistress' home. He had "come back" politically by getting himself elected to the County Commissioners' Board—but he was out for complete vindication. Now, he was running for Mayor.

Maschke was supporting William S. FitzGerald, who had been City Law Director in Harry L. Davis's administration. But even his support was not enough. Kohler won as the result of a methodical, doorbell-ringing campaign. He didn't make a single speech.

The day Kohler was elected he disappeared from the city mysteriously. Nobody knew where he was. Everybody was looking for him. Every paper, of course, wanted an interview.

The next morning—about three A.M.—I received a telephone call at home. A voice said, "Don't ask any questions. Take a train and meet me at Green Springs. Don't tell anyone."

I recognized the voice.

Kohler and I had been fairly good friends. He tried to browbeat most people, but I wouldn't be browbeaten. He liked that. I was also fair—or tried to be— and he liked that too.

I took the train and arrived at Green Springs in midmorning. I knew Kohler would be taking the baths there, and I waited for him outside the bathhouse. He showed up with a towel around his midriff, and a batch of notes in one hand.

"A complete list of my cabinet appointments," he said, offering no further comment.

I started to ask questions.

"Louie, that's all there is," he said. "It's a scoop. That ought to be enough for you. I'll show you where the phone is."

It was 11:30, and our home-edition deadline was creeping up on me. I hot-footed to the phone and gave the office the story.

A question came over the phone: "Where are you?"

I said I was not in a position to tell. They persisted and the Editor got on the wire, but Kohler was at my elbow, saying, "All bets are off, if anybody finds out where I am."

After I hung up, Kohler said, "Excuse me, Louie—I'm going to take a nap. I've got a two-year headache ahead of me." Two years was the Mayor's term.

I took the train back to Cleveland. When I walked into the office I found a note from the Editor.

"This is one of the biggest political scoops we have ever had," the note read. "It means $5 a week more in your pay envelope. But for God's sake next time tell us that you're going some place, even if not where."

In his time Kohler painted everything the city owned —including light poles—an eye-shocking orange and black, and put his name on every piece of city property. He was the most controversial political figure of his time. He was curt, rude, profane. He ridiculed officials and the public, saving his worst barbs for the "do-gooders," and manipulated every branch of the government himself. And when he died, better than a million dollars was found in his safety deposit boxes.

The Press ripped him, crusaded against him, and leveled its most explosive editorial artillery against him. In spite of this—and knowing not only that I wrote many of the paper's editorials, but that my opinion of him as a public official was worse than that which the paper expressed—Fred Kohler gave me more exclusive stories than any man who ever held public office in Cleveland. I was never to know why, unless it was because I never backed away from him. I simply stood toe-to-toe whenever he started his withering sarcasm or out-right profanity.

On one occasion, when I hung the phone up on him in the middle of one of his frequent explosions, he called back and gave me a good story. He didn't apologize. He just gave me the story—and then in the middle of it *he* hung up. Maybe he felt that evened things up. He was like that.

Chapter 15

I T WAS soon after I again became City Editor that, quite by accident, I bumped into a young man who was to do more to change the face of Cleveland than anybody else ever did. It was raining. The sky was black. The wind blew in gusts around the downtown building corners.

I had borrowed somebody's old umbrella. As I came across the street it took off. I tried to hang onto it, but the wind simply whipped it inside out. In my frantic effort to save it I crashed squarely into a man coming toward me and almost knocked him off his feet. He came up smiling.

"Things like that will happen," he said quietly.

"I'm sorry, sir," I said. "It was really an accident."

"Yes, of course," he said.

Then I realized that I had seen his face in our paper that day. He was O. P. Van Sweringen, the real estate man. He quietly acknowledged his identity, and we walked together across the street. He was headed for a hotel, and I for a streetcar.

"Someday," I said, "I would enjoy sitting down at lunch with you."

His eyes lit up in an amused way.

"If that's an invitation, I'll accept," he said. "What about tomorrow?"

We made an arrangement for the following noon.

That was the beginning of a combined professional and personal friendship which lasted as long as he and his brother lived.

From a farm near Wooster, Ohio, the two brothers had come to Cleveland, sold papers, got odd jobs, and then, as they walked across a plateau east of Cleveland, had a vision of a beautiful suburb. They realized their dream. The suburb became known as Shaker Heights— after the Shakers who originally owned the land.

Their success was phenomenal. They restricted a large tract of land, bought lots on credit, and sold at a profit. The project took hold in a big way.

In order to provide transportation for their 2,000-acre development, they tried to persuade the Cleveland Railway Company to extend its tracks. The company refused. That put the Van Sweringens—right then and there—into the transportation business. To get a mile of trackage needed to complete their right-of-way, they obtained control of the Nickel Plate Railroad from the Vanderbilt interests for a price supposed to be near $9,000,000. They were on their way.

I began spending considerable time with the "Vans." The two bachelor brothers were beginning to be Cleveland's No. 1 Story. They were dreamers, but they were also doers.

They moved their offices from the Society for Savings Building, in front of which I first literally bumped into "O.P.," to the Marshall Building, in more spacious and elaborate headquarters. They did everything with a flair, and well. They were perfectionists.

Some people have said that if Moses Cleaveland made Cleveland by founding it, the Vans remade it.

One day O.P. was looking out the window of his office on the tenth floor overlooking the Square.

"A very shabby skyline," he said. "Cleveland needs to change itself from an overgrown small town to a metropolis."

Standing there he outlined his dream for a great tower whose summit could be seen for miles around—surrounded by a group of buildings which would become the centerpiece of Cleveland.

"It will come someday," he prophesied.

"And when it comes," I suggested, with professional selfishness, "we would like the story."

He laughed, and said, "You will get it."

We did.

When his dream of the Terminal Tower for Cleveland began to take shape, The Cleveland Press got the first architect's picture of it. There was nothing on

Page One that day but the Terminal Tower that O. P. Van Sweringen dreamed of. It now stands majestically over Cleveland.

The Terminal Tower was formally opened on June 28, 1930, with a great civic celebration, including a luncheon in its concourse. Everybody who had any part in bringing it to fulfillment was there, with two exceptions—O.P. and M.J. Van Sweringen, the brothers who had really built it. I called O.P. at his home.

"Aren't you coming down for the opening lunch?" I asked.

"No," he said. "The weather is nice. I'm going to take a walk in the woods."

A few days later O.P., M.J., and I were walking up Euclid Avenue, Cleveland's principal street. It was noon, and the streets were crowded. A friend who had spotted me asked afterward, "Louie, who were those two nice-looking fellows you were with on Euclid Avenue yesterday?"

When I told him he was dumfounded. Few people recognized the brothers, now famous the country over. So little did they allow themselves to be seen in public that they were almost total strangers in the very city whose face they were almost completely changing.

The Van Sweringens were responsible for my leaving the City Editorship of The Press a second time, after I had been three years in the job. They were doing big things so rapidly that they became a beat all to themselves. Because of my known friendship with them it was decided—with my urging—that I take over this beat, and I covered it for quite a long time. With their help and blessing The Press published serially the only accurate story of their lives—with exclusive pictures they supplied.

The Van Sweringens had had a swift rise. They had an equally swift decline. The depression broke them.

At their peak, in 1930, they controlled upwards of 150 corporations, which in turn controlled: Twenty-three railroads, seven holding companies, one large coal company, four traction companies and one traction holding company, ten real estate companies. Among the railroads they controlled were the Missouri Pacific, the Erie, the Nickel Plate, the Chesapeake and Ohio, the Pere Marquette, and numerous smaller roads, such as the Beaumont, Sour Lake & Western and the Hocking Valley.

They were never idle a moment. They were always thinking, planning, dreaming. They were so sensitive that a slightly inaccurate statement about them brought tears to their eyes, but they could also fight like tigers. They led sheltered lives on a castle-like domain called Daisy Hill east of Cleveland.

The Van Sweringens in a very real sense were products of their times. They were geniuses who came to full flower at the moment when the physical growth of the country was most rapid—when mass production was phenomenally multiplying the industrial sinews of America. Perhaps they can happen again somewhere, but it seems doubtful. It is not likely that America will see duplicated in the future their incredible performance.

The tragedy of the Van Sweringens is that they, like

others presumably delicately attuned to the economic tides of America, did not foresee the great collapse that plunged the nation from the summit of prosperity one day to an economic crack-up the following day. Meticulously, thoroughly, comprehensively, the brothers had followed American business. They had a great corps of business economists and statisticians who met regularly to examine, to challenge, to forecast probable trends. It was generally assumed that the Van Sweringens, perhaps as well or better than most great financial and business organizations, knew the lay of the economic land ahead. It turned out—as it did for the wisest of the experts—that they didn't know.

I saw O.P. last not long before he died, when the wreckage of his meteoric career lay strewn across the American business landscape and there seemed to be no way of saving it. Ironically enough, in the midst of all this despair and reverse, again I stood with O.P. looking out over the Public Square. Time had changed his appearance, but it had not, even in these dark days, changed his outlook. Everybody but O.P. thought all was lost.

"It looks nice," he said, pointing out over the Terminal group, and at the network of tracks below. "It looks nice—and it looks permanent. It does make the city look metropolitan, doesn't it? We have much yet to do. We will do it."

He had been the central figure—with his brother—in some of the most bitter financial struggles in the modern history of the country. The United States Senate had at one time inquired into the struggle. O.P., quiet, reserved, calm by nature, fought hard, made enemies, made friends, made plans, made dreams, made money. But as the country began slowly to pull out of the depression, he died in his sleep on November 23, 1936, aboard a Pullman on the Nickel Plate Railroad as the train neared Hoboken, N. J. He was fifty-seven—and he still had many unrealized plans.

Whatever the mixed feeling about O. P. Van Sweringen in the circles where bitter contests are fought for control of vast properties, in Cleveland, where he and his brother fashioned a beautiful suburb, remodeled an overgrown town into a metropolis and changed the face of a whole city, there remains a friendly regard for him.

A year after O.P. died the Probate Court in Cleveland received a statement of claims and debts. O.P. had an indebtedness of $80,733,566.45 at the time of his death. His estate was appraised at $534,994.

The twenty-three-year-old City Editor who literally bumped into O. P. Van Sweringen for the first time during a wind-blown rainstorm has an additional appraisal: He helped Cleveland grow up. That civic asset—standing high over the revised Cleveland skyline —no depression or liquidators could take away.

Time has made legendary characters of the Van Sweringen brothers all across the land. The legend is strongest in the city in which they lived, fought, and accomplished. They did more, physically, for Cleveland than any one else ever has.

Chapter 16

MADISON SQUARE GARDEN couldn't accommodate another living creature of any size or category. The place was packed to the rafters, and this wasn't a figure of speech, for many people were actually perilously perched on them.

Ear drums were split by the noise. Cowbells, sirens, horns, iron clappers, baseball bats, dishpans, and noise-making instruments conceived by Satan himself had been gathered from all forty-eight States and the possessions for one maniacal purpose—to make noise.

Outside it was hot. Inside the heat was intolerable. People fainted. Tempers were short. Nerves were frayed. Thousands milled around, bumping, jostling, cussing at one another, parading, jeering, cajoling, gently beseeching, belligerently threatening.

I had never seen anything like this. It was a controlled riot, if such a thing could be. It was American democracy in full flower. It was the 1924 Democratic National Convention.

It was hard to believe that in this bedlam two men were to be nominated for President and Vice-President of the United States. Underneath all the pandemonium the bitterest struggle in modern American politics was taking place. The forces of William Gibbs McAdoo and those of Alfred Emanuel Smith were locked in a contest which has rarely been equaled at any time in this land of free political choice.

Some who came anticipated a battle. They did not expect a war. Some expected it to be hard-fought within the usual rules. They did not reckon on the claw and hammer, and no rules. The wisest had thought the convention might last three or four days. It was now in its tenth day with no sign of an end, either peaceful or bloody. And all through the July days and nights the weather had varied, if at all, only a few degrees from one day to another. Always the thermometer was within a margin of its mercurial ceiling.

I should have deplored all this. As a citizen of the country, I did. As a newspaperman, I didn't. As an individual, I was frankly delighted—for I had a special stake in the endurance of the convention and its eventual compromise. On what happened depended whether I had made perhaps the biggest scoop of my career or whether I was just another political prophet who had called the wrong turn.

My story goes back to a poker game better than ten

years before. It was an unusual poker game, not played for the usual pot. I was then a police reporter, working around the old Police Headquarters on Champlain Avenue.

Ed Moore was a Youngstown, Ohio, lawyer. He had a small practice, but a good one. His clients paid him well. They were mostly from the thriving steel mills of that city by the Mahoning River, and occasionally they got in trouble. Sometimes that trouble happened in Cleveland, and when it brought Ed Moore to town, he liked to stop in and play a game of poker with the police reporters. He had quite a reputation for the game, and it was reputed that he played for substantial money— but not with us. He knew our limitations, and the stake was always some bizarre thing that struck Ed's fancy. But on one particular night his idea was a little more practical.

"Suppose we play for a good story," Ed proposed. "If I win, I get a break from you sometime on something I do when I come up from Youngstown. All right?"

"All right, so far as it goes," I said. "But suppose you lose, then what happens?"

"Why, you get an exclusive story from me someday. All right?"

"All right," I said.

We shook hands on it.

The cockroaches, with which the reporters' room at the old station was infested, crawled all over the table while we played. We were accustomed to them, but they bothered Ed. He kept sweeping them away with a folded paper.

I had never cared particularly for poker. It was purely a game of convenience for me at the station. I played occasionally to pass the time with the police officers who stopped in at our room.

Ed won at poker most of the time. He loved the game and played with a flair, but this time he lost.

"All right," he said. "I'll pay you off someday with a good story, I promise."

The years slipped by. I kept in touch with Ed Moore from time to time, as I ceased to be a police reporter, and took on the assignment of writing politics. Ed became quite a political figure in Ohio, and, after a while, on the national scene as well. His influence was steadily broadening.

He acquired sufficient stature to be credited in 1920 with having almost single-handedly put over the Democratic presidential nomination at San Francisco for his fellow-Ohioan, James M. Cox, one-time governor of the Buckeye State. That was the time, also, that a handsome young Assistant Secretary of the Navy, Franklin D. Roosevelt, was nominated as the vice-presidential running mate for Cox.

So Ed Moore had become over the years one of the country's most formidable political strategists, and I was yet to collect the bet I had won from him in the old cockroach-infested police station.

With the convention coming up, I got in touch with Ed, about the middle of 1923. I knew if anybody could bring me up to date on behind-the-scenes maneuvers for the big battle ahead, it would be Ed Moore.

I called him on the phone.

"You happen to be coming up this way any time during the next month?" I asked him.

This was in August. The convention was still almost a year away, but in our business we work a long time ahead. Many a headline in a newspaper, even though it lasts perhaps for a single edition and then may be forgotten by the reader, is the result of long, tedious, meticulous work. Many sources have to be developed. Many friends have to be made. Much information has to be pieced together.

"Yes," Ed said, "I'm coming up tomorrow, in fact."

"Another client in a jam?" I asked.

"Yes, but I don't meet them in Police Court any more, Louie," said Ed. "I usually meet them in a bank, or in the civil courts."

We arranged to meet.

We talked for a long time. As I suspected, Ed Moore knew the whole background of the coming struggle between McAdoo and Smith.

"It's going to be a bloody one," he said. "This is going to be the worst knock-down-drag-out fight the country has ever seen. What's going to make it even worse is the undertone of religious conflict that will run through it. You going?"

I was. It would be the first national political convention I had ever seen.

"You sure are picking the right one for your first," Ed said. "I'll keep you posted. I promise. I may have that story for you, the one you won in that poker game. This might just be the time I can pay off."

The months passed. The middle of June came, and

the convention was only two weeks off when Ed Moore called me from Washington.

"You going to be in Cleveland Saturday?" he asked. I said yes.

"Meet me at the Hollenden Hotel," he said.

I met him there, and he gave me a detailed fill-in of the McAdoo-Smith behind-the-scenes fight, and who was leading each side.

"Now," he said. "I want you to call me one week from today. I think at that time I'll be in a position to tell you what's going to happen."

I didn't have to call him. He came up from Youngstown.

"Another client?" I asked.

"No, Louie," he said, "this time I came up for only one purpose and that's to pay off an old poker debt to a newspaperman." He then told me that neither McAdoo nor Smith would be nominated.

"Who will it be?" I asked.

"I know, and I know for sure, but I have to exact one condition from you before I tell you," he said.

"All right, Ed, what's the condition?" I asked.

"The condition," Ed said, "is that under no circumstances will you tell a soul as long as I live. I won't tell you, and furthermore I can't tell you, unless you promise on your honor to respect that condition."

I promised, and we shook on it.

Ed Moore was a rather small, well-packed, but not overly fat man, with a good sense of humor and an infectious personality—but he was in grim earnest about my promise.

"Louie, I'm going to give this to you," he said. "No other newspaperman will be getting this information from anybody else. I will stake everything on its being right. This is the way it's going to happen. But, remember, nobody is ever to know while I'm alive where you got it."

Again I agreed. Fate has now released me from that promise.

Ed Moore then told me that John W. Davis of Virginia would be the compromise nominee of the Madison Square convention. He said the convention would go much longer than most people expected, because the bitterness between the McAdoo and Smith forces—and also between the two men themselves—was so intense that intercession would be utterly impossible for quite a time.

"How will it actually come, then?" I asked Ed.

"Louie, that's all I can tell you now—just flatly and positively, and you can bet your life on it, John W. Davis will be it. The rest of it you'll have to attend the convention to find out."

I went back to the office and wrote my story. It forecast without any qualification that John W. Davis of Virginia would be the presidential nominee of the Democratic convention.

A hundred questions were thrown at me at the office. I stood by my guns, but I would not tell my source.

"It is the best source possible," I said, "and I'll stake my job on it."

The Press put an eight-column bannerline on the

story, as uncompromisingly flat as my story. When I saw it in print I broke out in a cold perspiration. No political writer was ever further out on a limb. If I was right, everything would be good. If wrong, I would make the paper look ridiculous—and myself as a political analyst even more so.

Three days later we packed up and went to the convention.

For months Marion had looked forward to going to the convention with me, but now she was getting more than even she had bargained for. She was having a good time of it, however. The heat seemed to bother her less than it did anybody else in the pine-benched press box packed with newspaper and magazine writers from all over the world.

The convention went on. Day after day the McAdoo and Smith forces battled for supremacy. The convention had opened on a bitter note. It went forward with increasing animosity. Every strategy failed. The deadlock was fixed, and neither side would budge.

In the long waits while convention strategists were trying, in restrooms and hallways and all sorts of meeting places, to swing the balance toward one side or the other, or to effect some compromise, the crowd kept up its characteristic din and hooting and cowbell ringing. The noise made our heads ache.

One thing that made Madison Square Garden endurable for us during those days was the fact that Marion was fortunately seated between two of America's most celebrated gentlemen. One was William Allen White, the famous homespun and courageous editor from Emporia, Kansas, a friend of ours. The other was Will Rogers, whom we now met for the first time in person, but whom we had many times seen spinning his lariat and making fun at audiences. Marion had the time of her life talking with these two mischievous celebrities, who did their best to distract me from my concentration upon my running account of the convention.

I had one serious conversation with William Allen White during those days. It was between ballots. The crowd had groaned when leather-lunged Governor Brandon of Alabama shouted out, as he had from the beginning of the convention, "Alabama casts twenty-four votes for Underwood," putting his whole emphasis on "UNDERWOOD!" This was, each time, the signal that the deadlock was still on.

Bill White had visited us in Cleveland some time before the Democratic National Convention. He knew how much we loved our home city.

"You kids still crazy about Cleveland?" he asked.

"More so than ever, Bill," I said.

"It's funny how a town or a city grows on you," he said. "Lots of people make the mistake of leaving a city once it has grown on them. They're never happy afterward. A lot of that's going on in America today. Even more of it will happen. You were born in Cleveland, weren't you, Louie?"

I told him I was.

"Any hankering to leave?" he asked.

"Not a bit," I said.

"My guess is you'll be invited to leave one of these

days," he said. "Somebody'll come along with a better offer. What'll you do then?"

"I don't know, Bill, for sure," I said. "But it would take an awful lot to pull me away."

He turned to Marion.

"Don't let this fellow leave Cleveland," he said, and added, "It's wonderful to make a career in the town where you were born. You get to know everybody. And everybody gets to know you. It's good to see folks you know grow up, have their families, make good. Even when you see some of them, unfortunately, fall by the wayside, oftener than not you can do something for them. You see some fellow who was poor at his school work get to be a big one in a bank or some business, and when he gets a little uppity socially you can bring him down a peg or two—or, if somebody pulls the aristocratic front you know he's just putting it on because his Pop was a peddler."

Suddenly changing his tone, he asked, "What was your Dad, Louie, before he started to write?"

"A carpenter, Bill," I said.

"I'm glad to hear you say that, Louie," he said. He put his arms around both of us and added, "You don't have to leave the family hearth to have all the pleasure that the world can furnish—it's right there in the family, and under that one roof."

As convention ballot multiplied into convention ballot, I sat on the pine-board bench, uncertain and apprehensive. Sometimes I would perspire heavily—and not from the heat. I even got a chill or two from the same sudden thought—the thought that perhaps Ed

Moore might have been wrong, honestly wrong, but wrong nevertheless, and that, as a consequence, having put my faith in him so unreservedly, I would be wrong.

The convention went brutally forward. The bitterness did not subside, and the noise seemed, if possible, to increase. The demonstrations became more frequent. Recriminations abounded. Men, otherwise friends, did not speak. Fist fights were not uncommon.

Then, one day whispers started. At first, they could scarcely be heard. Nobody gave them credence. Such reports had been kicked around before throughout the long convention.

This one, however, grew in volume, and belief, as the day went along.

"It's Davis," the whisper became louder and more insistent.

Newton D. Baker came out of his hotel. I had known him, of course, as Mayor of Cleveland, and he had been Woodrow Wilson's Secretary of War—the sole surviving valiant crusader for the Wilsonian concept of world peace.

"Mr. Baker, have you heard the Davis report?" I asked him.

"Yes, Louie, I have," he replied.

"Does it look good?" I asked.

"Better than any so far," Mr. Baker said. And then he added, "I can tell you who really knows."

I waited for him to identify that source.

He hesitated. Finally, Mr. Baker said, "Hunt up Ed Moore, and he can tell you all about it."

I thought I saw a twinkle in his eye, and for a fleeting

instant, I wondered whether Mr. Baker knew that Ed Moore had given me my original tip.

I went out to hunt up Ed Moore, and found him at the convention hall literally surrounded by delegates, convention bigwigs, and newspapermen. No chance to get to him now, I concluded. At that moment he looked over in my direction, and, with a finger, beckoned me to come over to a corner.

"It's happening right now, Louie," Ed said. "It'll be done before the day is over. I guess that pays me off," he said, with a gay smile, and lost himself quickly in the crowd.

Back home The Press took a picture of the front page that had carried my John W. Davis forecast, and put a caption on it: THE BIG SCOOP.

I clipped it out, and sent it to Ed Moore in a letter marked, "Strictly Confidential," with a penciled note across it:

"This belongs to you. Can I now tell how I got it?"

Ed didn't write to me. He called me by telephone the minute he received my note with the attached clipping.

"Louie, you made a solemn promise to me," he said, "and you must never, under any circumstances, tell where you got that story. Never," he sternly admonished, "so long as I live."

I promised again, as I had several times before, to observe faithfully our understanding.

And so, for many years, I never told how a kid police reporter's poker bet with an occasional Youngstown legal visitor paid off into one of the biggest political stories of the time. Ed Moore is dead, so here and now, in this book, I reverently pay my respects to an almighty good friend—a man who knew something very important was going to happen a long time before other people knew, and, to pay off his longstanding bet, let me in on it.

I never knew how Ed Moore happened to know. That story died with Ed Moore—and I don't think he ever told that one to another soul.

Chapter 17

IT WAS NOW 1926, and I was faced with the greatest crisis of my life.

The day Victor Morgan had hired me, eleven years before, as a $15 a week reporter for The Press, he asked me, "What are you shooting for in this business?"

"Your job," I answered.

He looked startled. I thought he might bounce me out on my ear.

"I hope you get it," he said.

To that purpose I dedicated myself.

For eleven years I had made the paper my principal interest. Long and irregular hours, hard work, difficult assignments—none of them mattered. I had thrown myself into my job almost to the exclusion of all else.

My family life had suffered, and I knew it. Marion knew it too, but she was willing to make her own sacrifices to help me accomplish my objectives. Our two children saw very little of their father at a time when they should have seen him most.

In those eleven years it had been my good fortune to do almost everything anyone is ever called upon to do in the editorial department of a paper—from cub reporter to every beat, every desk, every kind of assignment. At nineteen I had felt myself too inexperienced to be City Editor, and had asked to be relieved of that responsibility; now, at twenty-nine, I felt equally convinced that I was qualified for the top job on the paper.

But I didn't get it. Someone else did.

I was sitting at my desk just outside the Editor's office when the word came. I was so stunned that the editorial half-finished on my typewriter was blurred. I couldn't finish it.

My first act, of course, was to seek out Ted Thackrey, who had received the appointment to be the new Editor of The Press, and congratulate him. He knew how much I wanted the job he now was to fill.

"I hope there are no hard feelings," he said.

"None at all, Ted," I said.

"We'll work together," Ted said, putting his arm around my shoulder.

I walked back to my desk. Before me was the most important decision of my life. Only six months before I had declined the editorship of a big paper outside of Cleveland. Marion and I not only loved Cleveland, but we loved The Press—and we loved both in the way our kindly friend, William Allen White, of Emporia, Kansas, loved his little town and the newspaper which had become the national mirror of himself.

Many people believed, when Earle Martin abruptly left the Editorship of The Press, that I would logically succeed to his place. I was one of them. Ted Thackrey was Managing Editor of the paper, and I was its chief editorial writer, carrying the title of Associate Editor. It was generally assumed around the office while Earle Martin was Editor that I was second-in-command. Martin himself had assumed it.

In the two months' interim, during which the owners of the paper deliberated upon their choice, I was congratulated on all hands as the paper's new Editor. I did my best to scotch the rumor, deplored and ridiculed the idea, pointing out that, as the immortal Scotsman said, there is many a slip between cup and lip. In my heart, though, I had believed it would happen, and I was bitterly disappointed.

I went out of the office and walked along the street paralleling Lake Erie. I stopped at Nick's hat-cleaning and shoe-shining place, a favorite spot.

"I congratulate you, Louie," said Nick. "You the new Editor—I hear."

"No, Nick," I said. "I'm not the new Editor. Mr. Thackrey is the new Editor."

Nick's greeting was a foretaste of what I was to get all over the town in varied ways.

Information travels fast. I wanted to tell Marion before someone else did, and I went back to the office to telephone her. What words could I use to reassure her when I felt that I had just failed the biggest opportunity of my life? I called, but when she answered, I sat at my desk with the telephone open at the other end, not saying a word.

Marion's instinct for divining things had always astounded me, and now her voice came into the receiver:

"I know, Louis. Keep your chin up now. Worse things could happen to us. We'll make out all right."

She had been more practical about it, all along, than I, warning me not to build my hopes too high.

That night I found sleep difficult for the first time in many years. I went to The Press the next morning trying to put everything aside and concentrate entirely upon my work, but it was not easy.

In midmorning I received a telephone call. It was from Earle Martin, whose abrupt resignation as Editor had opened up the post now filled by Ted Thackrey.

"Can you have lunch with me today?" he asked.

Earle Martin had been a good boss, and I had worked hard for him. He was a great newspaper editor, resourceful, enterprising, and fair. I liked him.

Toward the end of the lunch, Martin, who was now publisher of The Cleveland Times, said, "I want you to come to The Times. I believe you would make the ideal Editor for our paper, and the people who own it think so too. We will pay you fifty per cent more than you are now being paid at The Press." And then he smiled, saying, "Of course, I know what you are making there—I signed the pay roll, remember?"

I asked Earle Martin to give me an opportunity to think it over.

"Take your time about it, Louie—only be sure you make the right decision," Earle Martin said. "This is really a big opportunity for you."

That afternoon I had a call from O. P. Van Sweringen who urged me to accept the offer from The Times. That night I talked it over with Marion, as I have always discussed every important decision with her. My mind was deeply troubled—but hers was clear.

"They are both wonderful friends," she said, when I told her about the offer from Earle Martin and the advice I had had from Van Sweringen. "But that isn't the question. The real question is whether we are going to run away from something. The Press has been good to us. They gave you your first real opportunity. Simply because you didn't get the Editorship right now when you thought it should come to you—and I thought so too—isn't reason enough to turn our backs on everything we've built up. You wouldn't be happy anywhere else. Your heart is in Cleveland and your heart is with The Press. I think our course is pretty clear, don't you?"

I did. The next morning I refused Earle Martin's offer, and I felt better. The decision had been made. I went back to work, my faith in The Press as a great, independent, courageous newspaper unaltered.

I was on a street corner several days later, waiting for a traffic light to turn, when I felt a light hand on my shoulder. I turned and saw Newton D. Baker. He was a small man, even slighter than I. He knew my great respect for him, for many times we had talked together

—or, rather, it would be more accurate to say Mr. Baker talked and I listened.

He asked me to stop in and see him, and that same afternoon I went up to the top floor of the building where he had his big law offices.

"Louie, I want to be direct," he said. "I want to talk with you about what has happened. I know it was a severe blow, but in the long run it will be good for you. Blessings frequently come disguised as adversities. It's a good thing occasionally to have your pride hurt, to be set back in something you want very much to accomplish, to be required to strengthen yourself, to make yourself better for the future."

I knew Newton D. Baker spoke from experience.

We talked for a long time about many things, but those were the words that I both appreciated and remembered.

"It will turn out for the best," Marion had repeatedly said. "You wait and see." And the next two years were for us, by the disguised blessing to which Mr. Baker had so wisely referred, the happiest up to that time we had ever enjoyed.

"The more we think of others," was another of Marion's favorite sayings, "the less time we have to think of ourselves." And she set me a constant example in courage, naturalness, humility, and compassion for others.

Long before this, Marion had begun to interest herself in welfare and civic work. She loved people. Any sick person in the neighborhood found Marion at the bedside. Her warm concern for others became first a neighborhood legend, and then, as those things happen, spread out around the city itself. One organization after another invited her to become interested.

Over the years, almost every women's organization in the community has seen her active in some capacity —and in World War II she worked into the small hours of the night, not for months but for years, helping to form a large group of women who supplied urgently needed personnel in hospitals, hotels, restaurants, offices, and other places. She has shown an astonishing ability to keep her home in meticulous order, take care of our children, and still make herself available for worthwhile obligations elsewhere.

I was happy to see her undertake these responsibilities.

From the time I had been a small boy it seemed to me that women ought to live more in the same world as men. My mother had devoted herself to her family to the exclusion of other interests. Father and his old cronies, as they sat around on our postage-stamp lawn on summer nights, used to debate, among other things, woman's place in the scheme of things. "Woman's place is in the home, tending to her children and her husband," they would say. Even as a small boy, not quite knowing why, I felt anger and resentment at their intolerance.

I didn't challenge Father then, but in later years we talked much about it. He eventually altered his opinion to some extent, but he lived too soon to vary his basic position.

Perhaps it was my intense feeling about my mother

and my wife that prompted me as an editor to fight vigorously for women's rights and their causes over the years. I have never overlooked a chance to do so.

I had seen too many homes in which husbands went off to work in the morning, lived in their work world, and returned home at night with no bond of interest for the wives who had remained within the four walls of the house all day. I never wanted to see Marion, either by design or unwittingly, shunted off into another world of interests. I wanted her to be in the world where I lived—and where I felt she, too, belonged.

At the office, under Thackrey's Editorship, I continued to express myself candidly, backing away from no one on what I believed. This put me at cross purposes many times with him. He agreed with me sometimes; sometimes he insisted on his own position. But even when I disagreed with him, I respected his courage, and we got along all right. After a time I became editorially so engrossed in certain big issues that my own interests and concerns were completely subordinated, and oftener than not forgotten.

Presidential politics became the big question. It was now 1928, and the big conventions were about to be held.

The first was in Houston, Texas, where the Democrats were once again faced with the question of nominating Al Smith. He had failed to get the nomination in 1924, when Ed Moore paid off his poker bet to me with the John W. Davis scoop. Davis had been severely licked. Now the Democrats appeared to be leaning toward Smith.

Houston, like New York four years previously, was hot. The convention this time, however, was held in a large tent. There was more air, a smaller crowd, less noise; and it was far more comfortable.

We had been there two days. This was the night that Franklin D. Roosevelt was to put Al Smith's name before the convention, and coin the phrase, "The Happy Warrior." The convention was excited. The press section was crowded. John H. Sorrells, who had been Managing Editor of The Cleveland Press for several years, and was one of my closest friends, was sitting on one side of me, and Marion on the other.

I was writing a story for the next day's paper, when I felt the pine table upon which I was typing out my story creak under a weight. I looked up.

Bending down toward me was Roy W. Howard, head of The Scripps-Howard Newspapers, owners of The Cleveland Press. The world-famous editor leaned close to me and, in what he intended to be a low whisper so that no one would hear, said, "Louie, I want you to come back by way of New York to see me. You are now Editor of The Cleveland Press."

Both Marion and John Sorrells had heard him, and I was instantly congratulated from both sides. I don't believe I even thanked Roy Howard for the appointment. Many things flew in a rush through my mind— especially my decision to stay with The Press for my own sake as well as the paper's, which was now so completely vindicated.

In New York, Roy Howard formally turned over The Press Editorship to me. He said simply, and with his characteristic emphasis, "It is your paper. Upon what you do with it, you rise or fall. Good luck!" He made no reference to the fact that I had been jumped over on the previous occasion. I respected him for that, as I have respected Roy and the Scripps family throughout my whole association with the Scripps-Howard Newspapers.

The Cleveland Press is the original of these newspapers. It was founded almost eighty years ago by E. W. Scripps, starting out as a militant and independent newspaper—The Penny Press. It has always been a militant and independent newspaper, owing allegiance to no one except the readers who buy it. From it grew the entire journalistic enterprise now known as Scripps-Howard Newspapers, and which also includes The United Press Associations, a world-wide news-gathering agency; Science Service, endowed by the concern's founder; and Newspaper Enterprise Association, which supplies features and editorial material to hundreds of newspapers and to radio and television stations.

My only contact with the paper's founder took place when I was a cub reporter, soon after Victor Morgan hired me. There was a big fire, and I rushed out of the office to cover it. As I came hurtling through the door, I bumped squarely into the protruding stomach of a large man. He grabbed me by both arms, harumphed, and said, "Young man what's your hurry?"

I was impatient. I had a story to cover. I said, "Let me go—I'm going to a fire."

He released me. Later, when I returned to the office, I learned to my momentary discomfiture that the stranger with whom I had so unceremoniously collided was E. W. Scripps, the paper's owner. He had told Editor Morgan about it, and asked to see me.

"Young man, I admire the way you didn't let anybody interfere with your work," he said, emphasizing his approval with a robust whack on the back.

In a measure greater than any other newspaper organization in America, the Scripps-Howard concern has traditionally accorded independent judgment to its individual editors. I was to make use of this latitude in the future, not infrequently to the acute distress of Roy Howard and others in the ownership and management of the papers. Their unswerving support, even when I am sure they believed me to be wrong, is one of the most gratifying aspects of my approximately forty years with Scripps-Howard.

My feet and mind had wings as I left Roy Howard's office. New York took on a new aura. Its skyscrapers, its parks, its teeming streets, its noise and confusion, suddenly became beautiful.

Marion and I walked up Fifth Avenue hand in hand like a pair of children. We talked and dreamed and planned, and looked forward to a future filled with excitement and challenge. As usual, she brought us both back to reality.

"It's going to be a big job, and it's going to take everything you've got," she said. "We're going to have to alter our way of living. The demands will be so much greater on you, and we'll have to do a lot of thinking about how we're going to manage ourselves as well as the business problems ahead."

It was a sobering thought, and I came abruptly out of the clouds.

Train time approached, and we headed back for Cleveland. Two weeks before I had left home as a combination political editor and editorial writer. Now everything was different.

Usually I slept well on trains—or anywhere, for that matter—but that night I tossed around the whole way. I wanted to get out and push the train faster. I wanted to get to work.

When morning came, and the train roared into the huge Cleveland Terminal, something hit me. All night I had wanted to get back home in a hurry. Now that I was here, I felt the challenge of my home town. Here I had to make good, or here I would be a failure.

Marion sensed what was going through my mind. She said, "We're home and we're going to make it go, aren't we?"

Somehow that was all I needed.

I headed for the office, and climbed the steps to the top floor. It was my thought to slip quietly to my old desk, get out my few belongings, and shift them into the Editor's desk without being seen.

When I opened the door leading into the Editorial Department, a loud burst of shouting greeted me. Everybody in the office seemed to be gathered there. They had put up some signs, and I was hit in the eye by one which read: "Try this on for size, Louie."

It was a small boy's cap. The point was clear. The folks around the office had plenty of ways to deflate any inclination toward cranial expansion.

We were all mostly young, and we had worked together for a long time. In a newspaper office nobody gets started very far down the path toward taking himself too seriously. There are many artful methods for cutting down to size.

After the unexpected mass welcome, I finally made my way to the office. Everybody had gone back to work, and I was alone.

In that solitude I thought of many things in a very few moments. Try as I would to put my mind on other things, images of people and situations tumbled around in my mind—people who had helped me—people to whom I was everlastingly indebted—people who over a long period of years had been good and kind and thoughtful.

The phone on my desk rang. It was Ray Huber, the Business Manager. Ray was a brusque man, but most of his brusqueness was pretense.

"Get to work," he called into the phone in mock severity. "Let's go!"

That brought me out of it. I went to work, and by the end of that first day I was completely exhausted. I had been on the phone most of the day. Problems came at me from every direction. People by the dozens came into the office.

One of the phone calls I had that day was from my friend, Newton D. Baker. Vividly I recalled that other occasion, when I had failed to receive the Editorship, and Mr. Baker had given me sound counsel that helped to lift my flagging spirit. I found time, as soon as I could, to go to see him.

After all these years, I cannot, naturally, remember Mr. Baker's exact words. But this is the gist of what he had to say—and I have never forgotten it:

> Louie, you and I had a nice talk when things looked bad for you a couple years ago. Now that things have looked up, I want to say some other things to you.
>
> A lot of people who haven't noticed you in the past are going to seek you out. They are going to make over you, flatter you, make you feel important. That, as you well know, is the way of the world. Many people gravitate toward position and power. They like to be identified with it.
>
> You managed to ride out a bad storm. It took a lot of courage, and you kept your sense of balance. You are faced with a different problem now. It also calls for keeping your feet on solid earth. If you take yourself too seriously, if you let people flatter you into believing you are a big shot, you are going to sacrifice the most precious thing in life—modesty, humility, naturalness.
>
> It is well to remember that most people will be around looking for you because you are now the Editor of a big and influential newspaper. Suppose, however, you were suddenly to leave that job. How many people do you think would run after you when you walked down the street? Very few. Perhaps, none.
>
> Always avoid confusing yourself with the office you happen to occupy. This will enable you to make better judgments of things and people, for one thing, and, what is even more important, to look at yourself in the proper proportions—uninflated, natural proportions. The decisions an Editor makes, the appraisals of people and issues he assumes to make, and the influence his paper exerts can only be as natural, as sound, as logical as he permits himself to be.

Between this counsel of Mr. Baker's, and the expert deflationary skills of my wife, who always kept me up when I was down and down when I had a tendency to soar up, my approach to the new world in which I was from now on to move was a relaxed one. I have never ceased being indebted to both.

When I got home that night my family had another surprise for me. It was not my birthday, of course, but they had all joined in baking a cake for me. It had part of Page One of The Cleveland Press on it—and what passed for a picture of the man who lived there. I never enjoyed a party more in my whole life.

Chapter 18

THE NEXT MORNING was different. The first
day's excitement was behind me. The future
was ahead.

"What kind of a paper should The Cleveland Press
be?" was the big question in my mind. "How can we
find out what kind of a newspaper we ought to publish for the people of Cleveland?"

From the moment I entered the newspaper business
I became subtly aware of a legend to the effect that
a good reporter is endowed with some sixth, or seventh,
sense. The notion prevailed that newspapermen are
"born and not made"—that the great newspaperman is
a man extraordinarily endowed with some kind of
divine omniscience out of which he unerringly does
the right thing at the right time, and with which he

intuitively senses not only what is happening but when and where and how things are going to happen.

This never seemed to me to make sense. After all, people's interests do change. A city grows. Its problems and requirements become different. A newspaperman could hardly afford to rely on mere instinct.

Modern facilities have made newspapers bigger. They have vast networks of wire services, syndicated features, and ready-made material from which to create themselves each day. But somehow I felt, as I became Editor of The Press, that modern newspapers had separated themselves from the people for whom they were really being published.

Questions were revolving around in my mind about the nature of a newspaper, what direction ours should take, what flavor it should have. I had suspected over the years that my knowledge of the city in which I was born and reared and had worked was rather limited. Now I had the feeling that my understanding of it was wholly inadequate, and mostly superficial. It was knowledge gained only by pivoting around in a very circumscribed area of the community—seeing the public officials, the politicians, the businessmen concentrated largely in the center of the town.

The easiest thing in the world is to drift into habit. Most people in our business restrict themselves to the downtown area of the cities, where their papers are published. They eat in the same places every day, visit with the same people, talk about the same things, and falsely assume that this represents the interests of their communities and the world in which they live—and for which they publish papers.

My office was, of course, located in the red-brick building at Ninth and Rockwell, where the paper was published each day—almost at the center of downtown Cleveland. Now I had another idea. It was to move my office out into the town itself. Not literally, of course— the paper would still be run from the desk where Victor Morgan had first hired me a dozen years before, and I would necessarily spend some hours a day there. But I wanted to move myself out—physically, for some hours of the day, and psychologically, to discover what was in the minds of the people of Cleveland.

I talked the whole matter over with Ray Huber. It is a common impression among newspaper readers that advertisers exert a great influence upon the editorial policies of papers—that they can, under the economic threat of their advertising dollars, get into a paper, or keep out of it, whatever they wish. The words of Ray Huber that morning, better than any I could improvise, set this straight.

"I believe you are right, Louie," Ray said. "What we don't know about the people who read our paper would fill more volumes than that library you keep on the fourth floor. We know so little about them it is painful to think about.

"We have got away from the people. They look at us as virtual strangers. They think we are in a cold business of publishing and selling news and advertising. They don't know us. We don't know them.

"They do not realize that the advertisers in our paper invest their dollars for only one purpose—and no other —and that is to move off of their shelves the merchandise they have there for buyers. They have no other purpose—and they should not have—and, for practical purposes, they don't have.

"You know what I would say to any advertiser who called me to ask that something be kept out, or in, simply because he paid dollars to us for space in this paper? I would tell him frankly to go to hell—and that would be the end of it."

Ray Huber is a straightforward, hard-hitting business executive, with a deep, abiding belief in the newspaper business, and a respect amounting almost to reverence for the sanctity of the editorial columns of a paper. I was blessed with him as a business partner. Later, when he was elevated to the General Business Managership of the Scripps-Howard Newspapers and eventually moved his offices to New York, I was again fortunate to have as his successor, John G. Meilink. Meilink was promoted from the Advertising Managership of the paper to Huber's key job, and he had, if anything, an even more pronounced regard for the editorial operation of the paper. Since he had been schooled under Ray Huber, he believed as implicitly that the success or failure of a newspaper centered around the caliber of the paper produced by the Editorial Department.

"You could spend your time no more profitably for the eventual strength of this newspaper than the way you are outlining," Ray Huber commented, in connection with my plan to move out into the city and try to find out what our readers wanted.

That was the start of a way of newspaper life I have never stopped. For months I left The Press office after some of my inevitable responsibilities had been discharged, and, putting my hat on, I went out into the neighborhoods, the stores, the saloons, the schools, the shops and offices of the town. Hour after hour I trudged from one to the other—asking questions, searching for information, trying to find out what people wanted or expected of their newspaper, what they didn't like, what they wanted more of, their current opinions about newspapers in general and our own in particular.

I had many interesting experiences. I had doors opened for me, and doors abruptly slammed in my face. One lady said, "I have heard of many ways that you slick salesmen have of getting into somebody's house but this one really takes the cake. Get out!"

She meant it, and the broom in her hand made what she said even more authoritative.

I still looked young, and I still found that sometimes people would not take me seriously. The bartender in a South East saloon looked me over with a distinctly hostile eye when I started to ask him some questions.

"Buddy," he said, "you ain't going to get anything to drink in this place for two reasons, because I don't think you got the money to pay for it, and because you're too young. So, on your way!"

In one factory I arrived just as the shift was being changed. This, I thought, was an ideal time to talk to some of the workers. I didn't get very far. The factory at that moment, without my being aware of it, was having labor trouble, and the foreman immediately tagged me as a labor agitator.

"Come on," he said, adding physical force at the scruff of my neck to his words. "Get out of here—and stay out! We don't want the likes of you around here!"

By and large, however, my experiences were altogether agreeable. I found that most people were willing, and in many instances eager, to talk about their newspaper—and that they had some very worthwhile ideas, criticisms, and counsel to offer. It took a long time—many months—but I kept at it persistently and methodically, visiting practically every part of the community.

Fragment by fragment, piece by piece, I gradually put together a pattern of what the people of my home town expected and wanted of their paper. I disproved, to a far greater degree than I had anticipated, the popular notion that people who work on newspapers automatically acquire the wisdom to decide what people want. I realized how completely wrong some of my own ideas were—how outmoded much of the thinking in newspaper offices was—how far the interests and the intelligence of people outstripped much of the material that was dished out for them.

I determined then and there that for the rest of my newspaper career I would keep my cruising range among the people who read our paper just as wide as time and energy allowed.

The basic thing I discovered was that people wanted a paper to be close to them, to be friendly—a paper that they could call on in emergencies and that would fight for them when they had trouble. I learned that the processes of government were so far removed from them that they couldn't get attention or action when they wanted something done—when they had a complaint to make or a suggestion to offer. I learned, likewise, that the thing people want most of all is attention, to be recognized, to have someone to call, to talk with.

The overwhelming percentage of the people with whom I talked had never been interviewed by a newspaperman before. Some of them had appeared in newspapers, in either the news columns or in pictures—and sometimes under adverse circumstances. With them I had to talk longer, to explain the ways of newspapers, why they did what they did, or thought they had to. Simply chatting and making a few explanations had the effect, in some instances, of removing bitternesses which had lasted a generation or even, in at least a dozen cases, had been handed down from grandparents to parents to children.

We at The Press were a relatively young group of men and women. We were not satisfied with our paper, and we wanted to strengthen it. That people bought the paper for the information it contained, the features it printed, the opinions it expressed, the way it did things, we knew. But we also were aware that all newspapers in one way or another did these things—that one newspaper might have access to one group of services while others had another kind available.

In addition to this, we knew, there was need for a unique and distinctive personality. E. W. Scripps had given The Cleveland Press that quality; others who had followed him had projected and extended it. But times change, and the personality and techniques of newspapers also are required to change. We felt that our paper in particular needed to change, to shift its emphasis, to adapt itself to today's requirements—and, most important of all, to get into it something of the human qualities that the people whom I had visited wanted.

Things like that cannot be accomplished overnight. To change a newspaper's sense of direction, to innovate, to experiment, to introduce new techniques and make the necessary revisions of basic approach requires time and painstaking effort.

We kept unfailingly open the line of communication with our readers. We invited them to the office. We visited them at their homes and offices and factories —many of us. We kept at it unceasingly.

At the top of Page One we put the paper's slogan— the slogan which directly resulted from pilgrimages out into the neighborhoods among the people themselves. It reads:

"The Newspaper That Serves Its Readers."

That is our heart, that is our purpose, that is our institutional determination. True, we must be basically a good newspaper. We must have upon our staff men and women of unquestioned authority in the many specialized fields that modern life in its complicated pattern has set up—like Real Estate, Pets, Science, Sports, Women's Interests, Gardening, Babies, Golden

Agers, and the many other interests covering the whole gamut of life from the cradle into the twilight of the years. But beyond this we want to render services to the people who come to us. We want them to come—to call us in an hour of need or crisis—to make us their friend—to turn to us when the impulse moves them—and to rely on us when they can get action or counsel in no other way.

Our office is constantly filled with people. They come to us at all hours of the day with all kinds of problems. They receive at our hands the warm consideration we have brought into our professional lives to give them.

People are quick to discern. They are quick to recognize the sincere from the spurious. They will not be deceived. You either feel for them or you don't. They either feel for you or they don't. It is just that simple.

This reciprocal relationship is not something that comes in a day—or a month—or a year. It takes many years, and the unceasing work of a total organization laboring in the same direction to bring it about.

Even though you were born in the city in which you have made up your mind to live all your life, it is not possible at any moment to say that you know it. You don't. Under the impact of the swift and steadily accelerating change that is taking place in a fermenting America, it is imperative, at all times, to keep at the business of knowing your home town. William Allen White had said it to me years before:

"You will never get to know your town as well as you should. It is always changing. People are born.

People die. The times are different. Their interests alter. Life goes on—but always in an ever-changing pattern.

"The change may be subtle. You may not always see it at first. You will have to stay with it, study it, know it, live with it. Even then, you many not know it altogether for what it is.

"Change on the other hand may be abrupt and clearly visible. It is then that you must be prepared to meet it squarely, head-on, not tomorrow, but today—the very moment you observe it. Tomorrow may be too late. People will not wait for you. You must be in step with them at all times—not too far ahead, not too far behind, but always in step. It takes a lot of knowing, and an everlasting dedication to the job of being with the people in your home town always, and forever."

Bill White was right, more right for today than for the time in which he said it, back in 1924—or than I then realized. I was to know as the years went forward that the editing of a newspaper is not adherence to any single pattern, created in and directed toward a single time. It is the endless, sometimes thankless job of keeping at the primary business of living with, understanding, and being sympathetic toward all people.

I was to learn, also, that people tend to ignore the counsel of a newspaper with which they have, as with any other business, a strictly cash-and-carry relationship—a newspaper which puts down the paper at morning or night with only a cold, impersonal treatment of the news and opinion of the day. With that kind of

newspaper people have only a fleeting and cold relationship. But with a newspaper which makes an earnest
effort to live with its readers, to serve them as perhaps
no other agency does, to anticipate their wishes, there
develops a friend-to-friend relationship. When that
kind of paper expresses an opinion or makes a suggestion, there is a far greater degree of friendly re-
ceptivity for it.

In a very real sense we started out to make The
Cleveland Press a paper which belongs to its readers.
Whatever is done is for them, and our main purpose is
to serve them in every way it is humanly possible to
do so.

We may print our paper at Ninth and Rockwell, but
we try to keep our offices out in the community itself—
not exclusively at the point where the papers roll off
the presses.

The Press has published a booklet for the people
who come to visit our offices, as we are happy always to
have them do. In it I tried to describe our paper—and
this is the way we all believe our paper should be regarded, both by ourselves and by others:

> The small boy waited nervously at the crossing for
> the light to change. In his arm he held fast the limp
> body of his black and white spotted dog. It was plainly
> sick.
> He looked up at the man also waiting. He said:
> "Please, Mister, where is The Press?"
> Where is The Press?
> It could be at Ninth and Rockwell. There is a build-
> ing with a sign at that location. The postal address is

there. Big presses, offices, trucks and the essentials of putting out a newspaper are there. Hundreds of men and women work devotedly under its roof.

The Press is there. It is also in many other places. It is in every home, in every school, in every industrial plant and office, in every church, and in every place where men and women and children—and small boys with sick dogs—live, work, play, think, dream and feel.

The Press is everywhere in Greater Cleveland. It has been so from the very beginning. The Press has had several addresses. It may have others, as it grows, in the future.

Its basic address will never change. It is "Greater Cleveland, Ohio, U.S.A."

The small boy with the sick dog at the street intersection knew that. He walked six miles to find his way to The Press. He had a reason. He knew that at The Press they cared. They cared for his sick dog, as The Press cares for all people in the great community in which for 75 years it has been publishing its paper for the people.

The test of editing The Press is simple.

It is:

"What is good for Greater Cleveland?"

Whatever is good for Greater Cleveland is bound eventually to be good for everybody—including The Press.

It is as simple as that.

Of course, it is not always as simple as that to search out what is good for Greater Cleveland.

To find out, The Press cannot stay at Ninth and Rockwell.

It has to be out with the people, living with them, sharing their problems, searching their hearts, their minds, their spirits and, in turn, reflecting in its columns what it finds there. It must walk with the people in their hour of problem and their hour of happiness, their hour of hope and their hour of dismay, their hour of planning and their hour of dreams.

The Press strives to be with the people, always at their side, always beating with their hearts, always fighting for what is good and against what is bad.

The Press' address truly is, has been, and always will be—Greater Cleveland, Ohio, U.S.A.

Chapter 19

I HADN'T BEEN Editor of The Press very long when I got into my first major piece of trouble.

On July 15, 1929, I stood before Judge Frederick P. Walther in his Common Pleas Court. At my side was Carlton K. Matson, Chief Editorial Writer of The Press. We were there as defendants.

The Judge had cited us for contempt and had decided he would sit both as judge and jury in his own contempt action. Matson and I were in contempt, he insisted, because The Press had published a few days earlier an editorial which had this caption: "If This Be Contempt."

The editorial leveled both barrels at the Judge because of a court order he had issued at the instance of a syndicate of gamblers who owned a Cleveland race track. The purpose of the order, we contended editorially, was to interfere with the Sheriff's obligation to do his sworn duty.

It was illegal to bet at a race track in Ohio. Yet betting was going on at this track, which the gambling syndicate had picked up for a song. The betting was not only in itself illegal; it was rigged against the betters. The Press smashed at the gamblers and the track. The Sheriff made a half-hearted attempt, under Press prodding, to stop them.

One Saturday morning I had received a telephone call from a long-time friend in city politics. In guarded tones, obviously talking where he didn't wish to be overheard, he advised me to have someone watch Common Pleas Court during the noon hour—particularly, he added, Judge Walther's Court.

Newspapers receive tips like that frequently. Some of them turn out to be valuable, other simply lead to wild-goose chases, but they are all checked. We sent a man around to Judge Walther's Court.

At noon, just before the Judge was leaving for lunch, attorneys for the gambling syndicate appeared. They asked the Judge to sign a writ, saying they were in a hurry. Their claim was that the Sheriff intended to wreck their race track. They advised the Judge, further, that the particular type of betting in progress at the track was conducted under an arrangement known as "the contribution system," which, they assured him, was perfectly legal.

The Judge apparently took the word of the gamblers' attorneys, for he said he didn't know about the situation personally. He picked up a pen and wrote a few extra words on the order which had been prepared and submitted on behalf of the gambling syndicate. In effect the Sheriff was ordered not to confiscate anything at the race track, unless the betting was "unlawful."

The Press blasted the Judge's order. In our editorial we described both the Judge and the Sheriff as pawns for the gamblers. In part it said:

> This judge issues an if-and-and injunction which is either monstrous, or ridiculous. If it enjoins the Sheriff from doing his sworn duty, it is monstrous. If it merely enjoins him from interfering with a legal enterprise, it is ridiculous. The law already protects legal enterprises.
>
> Undoubtedly, what the injunction amounts to is really a bluff. Some might call it a feint. Walther should know this, if he knows any law at all. The Thistledown gang certainly knows it. But the Thistledown crowd is trading on your natural lack of nerve, Sheriff. They figure that you won't stand up against a judicial injunction, no matter how much of a travesty it is upon its very name.

When our trial came up, the courtroom was so crowded that the doors had to be shut. It was filled with lawyers, clerks, reporters, shysters, legislators, councilmen, bailiffs, stenographers, prosecutors, fixers, loafers, and some of the gambling syndicate whose lawyers had duped the Judge into issuing the absurd writ.

The case instantly attracted national attention. Reporters from papers all over the country were there. William Randolph Hearst went to Page One on all of his newspapers with an editorial, from which I quote:

196

It is astonishing that in this Republic, which sought to abolish tyranny, there should still exist judicial tyranny, exercised through the power to punish for contempt of court. The tyranny of judges can be just as great as the tyranny of kings.

Hundreds of similar editorials were published.

Tempers flared in the courtroom. John A. Cline was chosen by Judge Walther to represent him. He was a sharp-tongued lawyer with whom The Press had tangled on many occasions. He was also quick, resourceful, and able. The Press was represented by my old friend and adviser, Newton D. Baker. The calmest and most relaxed man in the courtroom was Mr. Baker.

Cline argued that the law had been violated, that the Court had been made to appear contemptible in the public eye, and, therefore, that we, Matson and I, should be given the full limit. Mr. Baker argued that The Press had exercised its right to comment upon the behavior of public officials, including the Court, and that it was fair and justified comment.

The case took days. It took volumes of testimony. It took long and tedious examinations. The time came for the final arguments. Judge Walther adjourned for the day saying that the arguments would be heard when Court convened the following morning. The lawyers gathered up books and papers to prepare for the arguments—all except Mr. Baker. He simply put on his hat, excused himself, and said, "I'm going home and read a book."

Few in America equaled Newton D. Baker's avidity

as a reader. He had one of the most extensive personal libraries in the country. Visitors at his home used to joke about the fact that the contents of the hundreds of volumes stacked on shelves reaching to the ceiling had been transferred to the mind of so tiny a man. Reading was his sole relaxation.

I called his home at nine o'clock in the evening on the pretense that I wished to ask a question about the Walther case. Actually, I called simply to allay my misgivings. The case was important to The Press—and to me. I had been Editor only a short time, and already the paper was in trouble. Also, this was a big issue, and we felt that the underlying principle was too great to be jeopardized.

Mrs. Baker answered, and explained, "Louie, he fell asleep an hour ago with a book in his hand."

I asked what book it was.

"One of his favorites," she said. "Shakespeare's *Midsummer Night's Dream.*"

I didn't go to sleep that night nearly so peacefully, nor so soon, as Mr. Baker. I had my own midsummer night's dream. It was more like a nightmare.

The following morning I was in the courtroom early. Mr. Baker came in just before Judge Walther opened Court, and the Judge motioned to him to proceed with his argument.

Mr. Baker rose. He looked smaller than ever as he stood before the high bench, his thumbs tucked in the corners of his trousers' pockets. He had no notes. He had taken off his glasses. In a singularly calm voice, he then presented what lawyers all over America agree is the classic argument of modern times in behalf of a free press and free speech. In precisely phrased English, documented by innumerable cases which he called to his mind while on his feet, without resort to law book or note, the famous Cleveland lawyer held the entire courtroom—including Judge Walther himself—spell-bound for hours.

Mr. Baker based his argument upon preserving "the American prerogative of criticizing any, and all public officials, as long as there is no interference with justice."

"Originally," he explained, "chancellors were representatives of sovereigns, and to speak ill of the chancellor was to speak ill of the sovereign. There was a time in England when no man above the level of a dark cellar dared speak ill of Lord Jeffrey. Germany has the crime of 'lese majesty.' Italy prohibits any words of criticism directed at its ruler. But not so in a free country, unless it has the effect of hampering justice.

"Rigid application of the contempt laws goes back into the dark days of history, to the days when the judge was the representative of the monarch, and the public was efficiently gagged. The strength of the American government lies in the fact that citizens may criticize their officials to their heart's content, unless the criticism interferes with the performance of duty and the administration of justice."

Mr. Baker launched into an attack on gambling, and, standing before Judge Walther, he sharply criticized the Judge's order. He described the Judge as a dupe of his friends. When the Judge protested, Mr. Baker read into the record laudatory remarks the Judge had made about these same friends upon many occasions.

"There never has been such an injunction in the history of equity practice in this country," Mr. Baker said, his chin jutting out toward the Judge for the first time in the proceedings. "If you can produce anything like it, I will waive the remainder of the argument."

He asked the Judge to cite such a case. The Judge remained silent.

"Whether you know it or not, you were induced by the agitation of your friends to interpose the powers of this Court, the Common Pleas Court, between the Sheriff and the performance of his duty," Mr. Baker said, his voice rising in emphasis.

Judge Walther half rose on his bench to protest that he did not restrict the Sheriff in the performance of his sworn duty.

"Then," thundered back Mr. Baker, "you didn't do anything at all, and, therefore, the editorial was right on either or both counts in describing your injunction as 'monstrous' or 'ridiculous.' "

Judge Walther found Matson and myself guilty of contempt. He sentenced each of us to serve thirty days in jail and each to pay a fine of $500, and we were promptly whisked off to the County Jail.

By a curiously perverse circumstance, we had been criticizing the Sheriff editorially, not only for his half-heartedness in going after the gambling syndicate, but also because he had bought enough apple butter to feed twenty times the number of prisoners in his custody. We had thus made "apple butter" almost a household byword in the town.

When Matson and I were being booked at the County Jail, jail attendants shouted:

"Feed them apple butter!"

Mr. Baker came to our rescue before we were put behind bars, and we were released on bail. He notified the Court that he intended to take the case to a higher court.

We went straight back to The Press office. In the very next edition we carried an editorial under the heading: "We Would Do It Again." The editorial in part read:

> The principle for which we were fighting was that of justice. We made our comment in what we thought was the furtherance of justice, not its hinderance. We have made no retraction or apologies. We intend to make none.
>
> If we have to pay the price of thirty days in jail and $500 fine, we consider it a small price to pay in a fight for a principle. Journalism is still a profession. Considerations of right and honor make it that. There comes a time when a word of common honesty, without consideration of hazard, is the greatest contribution a newspaper can make to its community.

That editorial, no matter what the outcome of the contempt case, was our position. Not only was it our position in that case; it has been our position during all the time that I have had anything to do with the paper.

The case went to the higher court, and in a scathing reversal of Judge Walther his verdict of guilty against us was set aside. The decision of the Court of Appeals included the following remarks:

> Now the thought in the mind of the Editor of The Press evidently was that here was a situation which called for strong remarks; and one must admit that in the editorials they did give utterance to strong remarks—but when one thinks of a judicial officer exercising the strong power of injunction to prevent an officer, elected and sworn to enforce the criminal law— I say, when one thinks that a court grants an injunction against said officer performing his duty, one cannot help but think that such action did call for strong remarks.
>
> We think that the court erred in sitting in this case and in hearing the evidence. He could have plainly sent it to another judge. We think he was not in a fit condition to give unbiased judgment. He sought to wreak vengeance upon the plaintiffs. Whether the court's order was designed to befuddle the Sheriff's mind we don't know. Many sheriffs would have been befuddled by such a writ. The order was not worth the paper upon which it was written; and if the order was not worth the paper upon which it was written, then how could a comment, however severe, upon the paper, be contempt.

We had won our first major fight for a principle, since I had become Editor of The Press. It was by no means the last. It had been a hard one, but we had been brilliantly defended by Newton D. Baker.

There was an interesting sequel—one which was to test our ability to set aside personal feelings and to make our judgments exclusively upon fair and impartial considerations.

Judge Walther served out several remaining years of

the term during which he had cited us for contempt, and then came up for re-election. The Press was confronted with the decision of what to do. In the several years subsequent to his action against us Judge Walther had shown himself to be a good judge. He resisted pressure on several notable occasions where he might have yielded, which was proof to us that he was conscientiously doing his best.

Many people assumed that The Press would, of course, be opposed to Judge Walther's re-election in view of his action against us, and particularly in view of the vicious remarks he had made in open court about the paper and myself. However, his opponents were not, in our opinion, as competent as he. The Press endorsed Walther, and he was re-elected.

He came into my office after our editorial endorsement appeared, and said, "Louie, I don't know whether I will win or lose for re-election, but I want you to know this. The fight we had was good for me. I hope that it was good for you."

It was, as Judge Walther suggested, "good for" me. It was a lesson in fighting hard when the principle justified it; it was also a lesson in not letting that fight cloud later judgments.

Chapter 20

ONE AFTERNOON, perhaps a year later, a delegation of my fellow-townsmen visited me in the Editor's office at The Press to invite me to become head of one of Cleveland's health and welfare agencies.

They knew I was deeply interested in health and welfare. Several of them, whom I had known almost a lifetime, must have had some idea of the circumstances of my childhood. They couldn't, however, have known exactly what influences in my earlier life had contrived to bring about my interest.

Inescapably, as they talked, my mind turned back to a particular day in June when I was a boy in Cleveland.

It had been hot. After sundown a gentle breeze came

up, stirring the Japanese lanterns just enough to make an attractive and shifting pattern of light on the broad church lawn.

Everybody in the whole neighborhood was gathering for the Church Social. Although it was not supposed to start until nine o'clock, when it got good and dark, folks began to show up almost as soon as the sun settled itself below the horizon with a final burst of saffron and pink. The late shafts of sunlight matched the faint glow of the Japanese lanterns when they were lighted up for the evening. Joe Thiez's father touched the candle to each lantern from the stepladder which Joe and I held in position for him, proud that we had this much of a hand in the proceedings.

The laughter and excitement and shouts of greeting, as people made their way up the church steps to the elevated lawn, added to the beauty and color of the evening. It was fun to sit on the lawn in the dark and watch the colored lanterns turn various faces blue and red and yellow and green. Some of the boys looked like Indians, and the lanterns did funny things to the ribbons the girls wore, making the blue ones look green, and the yellow ones red. In the dark, we had a lot of whispered fun about it all.

Nothing for the Church Social had been bought in the store. That was a condition which the elderly Rev. Thomas Alburn had imposed.

"We'll have none of that already prepared stuff for this Social," he had announced from his pulpit a month previously. "All the proceeds will go, as usual, to the special fund to help the needy."

Cakes, baked fresh on the day of the Social, were arranged on a long, narrow table that stretched almost the whole width of the Church lawn. On another table nearby was a mountain of assorted sandwiches. But the children tended to linger most of the time where the ice cream was set out. We couldn't see it, but we put our noses close enough to the home freezers to know just what kind it was, vanilla, or chocolate, or strawberry, or even Mrs. Hahn's orange ice cream, for which among the neighborhood children she was especially noted. In the homes where the ice cream had been made that day the children had been required, as their contribution, to work the freezer, turning the handle for endless hours throughout the whole afternoon.

We raced from one table to another, and our tumbling itinerary took us, of course, to the booths around the end of the lawn. The booth where Mrs. Noss was telling fortunes from tea leaves and cards picked at random from several decks was the most popular for the grown-ups, while the children favored the section roped off for a "fishing pond." There, for a penny apiece, we dipped rods with large pins at the end into a square of "water" and drew up as prizes rainbow balls or little dolls or colored books.

It was always Reverend Alburn's custom to announce the amount of money taken in at the Social just before he said the "Goodnight" which brought the occasion to an official end.

"My friends, this is the best Social we have ever had," he would always say, raising his hand for silence. We all stopped, and listened.

"We have this evening put together the sum of $164.08 for our fund," he went on. "And once again, I express to you my appreciation for the confidence you repose in me to distribute this money in any way that I see fit. We have all had a very pleasant evening, and we have all done good work in God's name. Let us now all kneel wherever we are, and send our thanks to our Common Father."

It was a wonderful sight, as the colored lanterns, stirred by the breeze, cast their soft reflections on the kneeling people and their bowed heads.

And then we all parted, talking and shouting, Reverend Alburn being the heartiest of all in his interminable goodnights to everyone who attended the Social.

I had not expected this basic question of civic participation to come before me quite so soon after assuming the paper's Editorship. Now I had to make a decision, one way or the other, that would in all probability affect my activities for the rest of my life.

In our business there has been a sharp division of opinion as to how much an editor and his associates should participate in a community's affairs. One side of this argument holds that an editor cannot maintain complete objectivity of opinion upon matters in his community if he himself becomes a participant. His role, this argument holds, should be exclusively that of an observer and a commentator, and such influence as he may exert should be confined to the columns of his newspaper. Some of the country's most famous editors have adhered unswervingly to this basic premise.

Many now do, although not, I believe, in quite so pronounced a measure as formerly.

The other side of this argument—and the one to which I cast affirmatively my lifetime vote—holds that an editor should evidence, both in his columns and in person, the deep interest he feels for the community in which his newspaper is published.

Now I was faced with the clear-cut choice of following one course or the other. I asked the delegation for several days of grace in which to think the matter over.

To one of them, a lifelong friend, I confided my quandary. "Once I take on this responsibility it will open the door, I am sure, to others which inevitably, in the nature of things, will follow," I said. "I can now say no and stand by it in all situations in the future. Then I will relieve myself of many responsibilities, burdens, and possible headaches, to say nothing of misunderstandings and misinterpretations of my motives.

"However, if I follow this course of nonparticipation, I will, I know, forever after be reproaching myself, always feeling I should be doing more for my home town. I am afraid I will consciously create for myself a spiritual vacuum. How can we, as a newspaper, ask other business leaders to assume their full share of civic responsibility, if we ourselves decline to take ours?"

I was thinking particularly that The Press had been founded by Mr. Scripps as Cleveland's newspaper, to serve this community and its people.

My friend said, "Have you not actually already decided then by what you have just said?"

"Not entirely. There is my professional status to consider. What about the argument in behalf of objective detachment from all these matters, the better to express one's self in his paper?

"What, also, about the receiving in confidence of vast quantities of information which, as the participating head of the organization, you cannot conscientiously make available to the newspaper of which you are the editor? Where in such a situation does your primary obligation turn?"

For the moment my friend was stumped, as I was. It was a bigger question, he agreed, than it at first seemed.

In considering the whole problem, I couldn't quite get out of my mind the recollection of Rev. Thomas Alburn. It was a long distance from his Church Social to the vast, intricate, and efficient health and welfare services of a big city today. Yet, I remembered how Reverend Alburn moved among the people in his whole neighborhood, regardless of whether they were his own parishioners, and became acquainted with them, their problems, their hopes, their needs, and the crosses all human beings carry in one way or another within themselves. He did not permit anyone to know whom he was helping, in what way, or by what amount. He had warned his congregation specifically, "I will on some occasion help some family not a member of this congregation. I will do it in God's name—and yours."

Reverend Alburn made his own research. He satisfied himself about a need. He then put money in an envelope and mailed it to the family he had decided needed help. To make sure his conspiracy of anonymity was absolute, he mailed the letters from different locations throughout the community.

One winter, shortly after the bleakest Christmas we ever had, an envelope came to our house containing only a ten-dollar bill. We were completely mystified by the white envelope and its contents, but I know now that Reverend Alburn must have learned about our family problems from some source.

That Christmas the worst blizzard in many years had struck Cleveland. The winds howled for several days. The snow came down steadily and piled up faster than it could be shoveled away.

On the night before Christmas, Mother gathered us together around the potbellied baseburner in the kitchen and warned us that Santa Claus might not stop at our house that night. She sent the other children to bed, huddled together to keep one another warm, and told me to stay up a little while longer.

Mother and I worked for several hours threading popcorn on long strings. Mother colored some of it pink by putting it in a pan in which she had melted some red candy that she had kept hidden away. The tree we carried in from the back porch had been brought to our house that evening by our friend, Mr. Belz, and was no higher than I was. By putting it on the kitchen table, Mother made it look quite big and beautiful. She fashioned a six-pointed star out of a piece of cardboard painted with water colors she took from our school kits.

The next morning Mother bundled me up with Father's big muffler and his big gloves, and I set out in the blizzard to borrow twenty-five cents from Uncle Bill Nassano—not for toys, but for food. I never forgot that Christmas—nor Rev. Thomas Alburn's plain envelope which arrived soon afterward.

We were a cosmopolitan neighborhood. No home was rich. None was even well-to-do, with the possible exception of Carlton Hahn's father who seemed to have a steady job. Carlton always had toys, but he always shared everything he had with the rest of us. There was a friendly neighborhood spirit also among the grown-ups—the spirit of helping one another out in sickness or in need. Even as children we shared it.

As a cub reporter I saw the health and welfare activity of the city begin to take shape. When the Community Chest came into being in Cleveland—pioneering in this remarkable concept of community-wide consideration for others—I covered as a reporter its very first meeting. I was deeply impressed by it.

The Church Social of Rev. Thomas Alburn had grown in my mind into an attitude, a perspective, and a basic, enduring interest. The principle behind the Church Social itself had grown as the community grew —as it became essential to have men and women educated and trained for social work—as it became evident that frequently the need was for more than material assistance.

The Church Social is still a great American institution. It is to be hoped that it always will be, that there will always be the Rev. Thomas Alburns of his faith, and other faiths, who guide their congregations to the humanitarian purpose which makes people better in every way. But in the broader sense, the Church Social of the Japanese lanterns strung out over the lawn on a scorching June night has given way to the great health and welfare activity for which America is widely noted.

Probably I do not need to tell what my answer ultimately was to the delegation which came to my office back in 1930. I accepted the welfare post they offered me. I chose a kind of existence about which there may be journalistic controversy, but from which many human and even certain professional satisfactions have been gained.

My identification with an infinite variety of organizations has proceeded in ever-expanding proportions during the approximate thirty years of my Editorship of the paper in my home town. These activities have required extra effort, extra hours, extra thought. They have intruded—if the word can justly be applied to something you enjoy doing—into such hours as might otherwise be reserved for home life and leisure. They have made both my wife and myself available at all hours and all times to a multiplicity of inevitable demands. We have been exhausted, frequently troubled, often wished we had never taken that first plunge headlong into the life of our home town. These, however, have been fleeting moments. From nothing else could I have gained such indispensable insight into the community in which our paper is being published—and for which, after all, it is being published.

There is also a strictly selfish reward. It comes, not with recognition of any kind, but from doing whatever, as a citizen in the greatest land on earth, one is able to do. It is the reward of just feeling good.

And to those in our business who insist that an editor's place is strictly in an objective cubicle surrounded on all sides by complete detachment from the readers of his paper, may I most respectfully suggest—if it is not already too late—that they try the other for a while. If they do, I assure them from happy experience they will realize what they have missed.

Chapter 21

THE MORNING of April 26, 1933, started out as a dull news day. Not much was happening. The telephone on my desk rang and I recognized the voice of a friend, who asked, "What about the Cleveland Trust Company?"

Since the Cleveland Trust Company was not figuring in any news situation, I countered, "What about the Cleveland Trust?"

That was the first intimation I had that there was a run on the bank. It was then eight-thirty o'clock. The bank had not opened. Yet many people had gathered in front of its branches and around its main office in the very heart of downtown Cleveland—at what is regarded as one of the world's busiest corners, East Ninth and Euclid Avenue.

Nothing throws a shudder into a community like a run on a bank. And, generally, nothing presents a newspaper with a more serious problem. But the specific problem presented by the run on the Cleveland Trust Company in 1933 was unlike any other I have experienced.

From some mysterious source a rumor started about the Cleveland Trust Company. It was then, as it is now, Cleveland's largest bank. It was as sound that day as it is right now, and it is regarded as one of the soundest banks in America. Yet like a prairie fire the rumor went around Cleveland, and depositors began gathering shortly after daybreak.

All during the morning the crowds multiplied, and the bank, and all its branches, paid out money. It was thought that prompt and unquestioning payment of depositors in full would bring the run to a stop. It didn't. The run continued, and it grew worse as the day went forward. By noon its proportions became so serious that emergency measures were thought to be imperative.

At this point our problem as a newspaper became acute. With our afternoon edition approaching, we were faced with the question of whether to say anything about the run or not, and, if we decided to do so, what point of view we should take, how much we should say, and what display we should give it.

It was our decision that a situation like this could not possibly be ignored. We had to take note of it in our paper, and the best course seemed to be simply to publish a strictly factual story, telling how the mysterious rumor had brought about the run in the first place and describing its gradual growth and the action taken by the bank's executives to reassure its depositors. This represented the combined judgment of our paper's key people.

In the midst of this conference I received a telephone call from Harris Creech, President of the Cleveland Trust Company. I had talked with him earlier in the day, assuring him that our staff as a group or I as an individual would be available if we could be helpful at any stage of the emergency. Harris Creech's call was in response to this offer. He asked me to come to his office, and it took me only a few minutes to get there.

Because I felt that my appearance at the bank might be misinterpreted, in this highly emotional and tense atmosphere, I went through a side door, and thus, in a labyrinthian fashion, ultimately arrived at Harris Creech's office on the fourth floor.

The president and the bank's other officers were anxiously gathered in a large directors' room. Every device they could think of had been employed to halt the unaccountable run on the bank, but it continued.

Harris Creech was a cautious man. The very qualities which made him so thoroughly dependable as a banker unsuited him for the measures now needed to stop this dangerous state of affairs. He outlined in detail, and in sequence, the day's efforts to bring order and calm into the atmosphere of potential catastrophe. The staff had offered many suggestions, but for one reason or another they had been set aside.

It was a tough spot. The bank's statement showed it

to be in excellent condition, and it was fully capable of paying out the money the depositors asked for—yet it was in imminent danger. It seemed to me that only a drastic measure would work.

Finally an idea occurred to me. It was an idea centered around Harris Creech himself, and it would work only if he agreed to it. I knew his temperament, but there are times when a man will, in an emergency, set aside all timidity and rise to the realities of a serious occasion.

I asked for a typewriter. This in itself would probably have astounded the bank officers under normal circumstances, but they showed me into an adjoining office, where I sat down at some stenographer's desk.

Two things, I believed, were essential at this moment. The first was a statement from the Governor of the Federal Reserve Bank, located in Cleveland. I called E. R. Fancher, who held this office, and told him where I was and what was in my mind. He in turn called Washington and talked with W. H. Woodin, Secretary of the Treasury. In a short time Mr. Fancher called me back, reporting that he had the green light to go ahead.

While I waited on the telephone, he wrote out in longhand a statement which he then dictated to me. I took it down on the typewriter. It said:

> Anxiety concerning deposits in licenses in Cleveland is unwarranted. These banks were licensed and re-opened for full operation after careful determination of their condition. They are sound and they have, and will continue to have, the full support of the Federal Reserve Bank of Cleveland.

These banks are deserving of the fullest confidence
of their depositors and of the entire community.

After finishing Mr. Fancher's statement, I wrote out
another brief statement. This one said:

I am Harris Creech, President of the Cleveland
Trust Company.

Unfounded rumors have been circulated about the
Cleveland Trust Company, causing many depositors to
withdraw their money. In order to accommodate them
to do so this Bank will remain open until 5 o'clock
instead of 3 o'clock, the usual closing hour, and will
open tomorrow morning at 9 o'clock.

I then took the statement in to Mr. Creech, wondering how he would take my suggestion, as I explained,
"What this situation needs, Mr. Creech, is a direct word
from you as head of this bank. I would like to suggest,
therefore, that you in person go to the lobby downstairs, climb up on a counter if necessary, and read this
statement yourself to the people who are there."

Harris Creech and his associates were obviously
startled. They looked at each other, and talked back
and forth for a bit, then Mr. Creech finally said, "We'll
try it."

Harris Creech was a thin, quiet, almost shy man,
earnest and sincere in both appearance and personality.
To do what I had proposed was perhaps the last thing
he would ever have dreamed of doing. But he did it.

In a lobby filled with depositors, pushed and crowded
by a line of people outside waiting to get into the
bank, Harris Creech gingerly climbed up on a counter.
He asked for silence and got it instantly.

In clear, ringing words, surprising even to his closest friends, he read the brief statement, and then the statement issued by Governor Fancher of the Federal Reserve Bank.

The crowd listened. Mr. Creech climbed down from the counter. This was the fateful moment. The crowd could go either way.

Harris Creech was prepared to stay in the lobby with his depositors as long as they wished him to. He was surrounded by people asking questions, and stoutly he answered them.

Presently, a few of the depositors put their bank books in their pockets and walked out. Others followed them. Within a short time the crowd thinned out, and a feeling of stability replaced the feeling of tension. Even before Harris Creech turned to go back upstairs to his office he knew, and everyone knew, that the bank run had been stopped.

It was a long chance, and it had succeeded simply because it deserved to succeed. A sincere man speaking in the lobby of his own bank, whose condition was among the best in the nation, was believed because he spoke the truth.

No one ever knew how the rumor started which prompted the run. The Government sent in Secret Service operatives who searched out every shred of evidence. Already, even on that fateful day, they were mingled among the depositors who lined up before the branch banks and the main office downtown, but they couldn't piece together anything at all. It was all hearsay; one person credited somebody else with hearing the rumor from another, and yet another. The background, of course, was the national "bank holiday" which had forced the closing of banks throughout the country, combined with the fact that several banks in Cleveland had failed to reopen. The only reasonable conclusion seemed to be that a malicious rumor had been thrown as a spark into the minds of an inherently apprehensive banking public.

That is one of the days I shall never forget, out of all the days of my newspaper career in Cleveland, because its potential for harm to Cleveland was great. The idea that came to my mind in Harris Creech's office that midafternoon was not particularly original, but it was, as it turned out, an effective one—made so by the character and reputation of a great bank and the sincerity of its president.

Among the precious papers I have preserved are two handwritten notes—one from Harris Creech and the other from E. R. Fancher. Neither is a fine example of penmanship, but these two almost illegible notes stir memories of one of the dramatic days of a lifetime.

This story of the run on Cleveland's biggest bank makes painfully familiar reading, perhaps, to those who lived through the tumultuous decade of the thirties. The stock market collapse of 1929 occurred only a year after I was made Editor of The Press (for the coincidence of which I disclaim any personal responsibility) plummeting the country from its high economic plateau of "prosperity forever" to the worst despair the nation had experienced in modern times. It brought along with it an apparently unending chain of social and political experimentation which caused sharper cleavage with a relatively conservative past than at any other time in the nation's history.

The newspapers of America, ours of course not excepted, had to display editorial flexibility and improvisation not theretofore equaled. From the standpoint of practical operation, business fell off, circulations subsided, and costs required serious retrenchments.

The primary test of any newspaper organization is its ability to adapt itself, not only to sudden emergency in a given hour or day, but even to unexpected change in the fundamental pattern of life. The shift from prosperity to depression, and, in the next decade, from peace to war, are extreme examples, but they dramatically illustrate the problems of change. Both required extensive readjustments of purpose, techniques, and emphasis. Both necessitated an almost immediate flow of new ideas, of enterprise, of ingenuity, especially in a business which is so highly competitive as is that of daily newspapering. During the depression, The Press editorial operation distinguished itself in a way which brought pride to my heart.

Early in my experience as an editor I contrived a simple formula by which to judge the underlying vitality of our organization. It was this: If the people upon whom I depended outthought me, created more ideas than I was capable of developing, and were abler and more resourceful than I, then I felt reasonably sure The Press was in sound organizational condition. Otherwise, I became restive and uncomfortable about the paper's health. By the grace of good men and women, and the further good fortune of having them, the latter moments have been relatively few during the approximate thirty years that I have had the editing responsibility of our paper.

There has always been in our office a free and easy exchange of opinion, constructive criticism, and ideas, and that's the way we like it. Not infrequently is the Editor overruled in none-too-gentle terms by others on the paper, and this is as it should be. There is no purpose in having able men and women on a newspaper only to have their effectiveness neutralized, as too often is the case, by an editor who insists, by some singular appropriation of divine omniscience, that he alone has the answers.

The Cleveland Press is not the reflection of a single individual. It is the reflection of many men and women —and it will be that way so long, at least, as I am responsible for it.

Chapter 22

ON JULY 11, 1935, the headline in The Cleveland Press read:

"The Press Urges Frank J. Lausche to Answer the Call of the City of Cleveland in Its Hour of Need."

City politics were in a mess. A clean, able, hard-hitting young man was needed as Mayor, and Lausche was, we were convinced, the man. His four-year term on the Municipal Bench had two more years to go. The Mayor's election was a few months away.

The editorial occupied the whole upper half of Page One. In big black type, it said, in part:

Frank Lausche is The Cleveland Press's choice for Mayor of Cleveland. We urge him to be a candidate. He is now a Judge on the Municipal Court, where he has proved himself fearless, honest, humane and gifted with a fine intelligence. He is young, and has all the vigor and enthusiasm of youth. He is a man of the people, born in Cleveland, raised in Cleveland.

He knows all the problems of the common people at first hand. He is a man of social vision. He is a man who can be counted on to look at every public question from the standpoint of how it affects the welfare and security of the masses of the people.

He has never been afraid to challenge the organization when he thought it was wrong. He has never hesitated to criticize the organization leaders. He has flatly refused to do what he thought was improper. As a candidate for Mayor, he could seek the office as an independent, as a citizen seeking the support of all citizens who want good government. . . .

Into a city torn by lawlessness and violence, ridden with graft and spoils-politics, infested with racketeers and plug-uglies, uncertain about its civic policies, needing a clean and honest and able leader—

Into these circumstances there would step this 40-year-old man, in the full bloom of vigorous and intelligent manhood, as the hope of this community when it most needs hope and help. This is the kind of man Frank Lausche is, and The Press urges him to answer the call of the city in its hour of need.

I had first seen Frank Lausche in action about a decade before, in September of 1928, to be exact, when I decided to drop in on a meeting at the Slovenian National Hall on St. Clair Avenue.

The man at the door stopped me.

"Where do you live?" he asked.

I was surprised at the question, and tried to avoid answering it.

"This is a neighborhood meeting," he explained. "We want only people who live here."

Frank Lausche Would Make Best Mayor

AN EDITORIAL

[newspaper editorial text]

Block Police on Truck Tribute

Unions' Threats of Picketing Fail Drivers

Tail of Hurricane Whips Cleveland

September 25, 1941

For Good Government---Nominate Lausche, Herbert

AN EDITORIAL

May 5, 1944

A Note of Regret

Leadership Needed

May 15, 1953   March 7, 1955

Louis B. Seltzer backs him, but not blindly

THE CELEBREZZE STORY

Celebrezze Is Man to Get Things Done

September 25, 1953

Smash Boss Rule--Vote for Celebrezze

September 28, 1953

Mayor Anthony B. Celebrezze and Louis B. Seltzer (1954)

The small hall was already packed. I was intentionally late getting there, because I wanted simply to slip into the meeting unnoticed. The meeting itself didn't interest me, but the man who was expected to speak did. I finally talked my way past the man at the door, and found a place standing up among a lot of other people who had apparently, like myself, arrived late.

My interest in this man had been stirred by several friends in Cleveland politics. One said, "Sometime you ought to take a look at this young Lausche fellow in action. He looks good."

At that time I had been Editor of The Press only a few months. I was then thirty-one, and the tall, athletic, handsome man on the platform didn't appear to be much, if any, older. He was, as I later discovered, thirty-three.

The meeting centered completely around him. He was urging the people to band together to protect their neighborhood, which was not far from the downtown district, from the adverse changes which were taking place in similar areas. He spoke eloquently, impatiently brushing back the thatch of curly black hair that kept getting in his eyes.

The crowd cheered him repeatedly, as he talked alternately in English and Slovenian, and the neighborhood organization he proposed was enthusiastically accepted.

I waited until the meeting ended. Threading my way through the jostling crowd, I finally reached him.

"I came out here especially to see you on your own ball diamond," I said, as I told him who I was. He laughed. "They tell me you've made yourself quite a figure out here," I went on.

I arranged to meet him at my office a few days later, and as we talked, my favorable impression of him was reinforced. He expressed himself in a straightforward way on some of the important current issues around town; and I too became convinced—as others had suggested to me earlier—that he was a good man to watch.

The Lausche family had come from Yugoslavia, his parents having been born there. Frank himself was born in Cleveland, and grew up in the neighborhood where for the first time I met him. He went to the public schools in that section of town. He played sandlot baseball in Cleveland, and worked as a lamplighter, in his father's small print shop, and at whatever else he could to earn money. Before he was eighteen he was playing amateur baseball with one of the city's outstanding teams, and had been given tryouts with semipro teams in Lawrence, Massachusetts, and Duluth, Minnesota.

He enlisted in the Army in World War I and was sent to Camp Gordon, Georgia, where he was given a chance to go to Officers Training School and, also, to play second base on the Camp Gordon team.

When Frank got home from the Army, he decided he wanted to study law. First he had to complete his high school work, which he did at the old Central Institute, and then he enrolled in night law school. In 1920, he was admitted to the Bar. He got a chance to practice in the law office of Cyrus Locher, who was at the time one of Governor Vic Donahey's associates. It was this association with Locher, and his own background in the Slovenian ward of Cleveland, that drew him into the Democratic Party.

Before he finished his law course, Lausche became interested in ward politics, and he was successful from the very start. He was not quite as successful, however, when he first tried for public office in his own behalf on a community-wide basis. His first two attempts to get himself elected to the Legislature ended in dismal failure. It wasn't long after his second attempt that I had gone out to the Slovenian National Hall to take a look at this young fellow who was supposed to be so promising.

We got to know each other fairly well during the next few years. In 1931, Lausche's first good political break came. The Republicans had held local power securely for a long time, but the tide was then turning for the Democrats.

The Cleveland Press had been impressed with Ray T. Miller, a fiery young county prosecutor who had ably handled some tough cases, and in an editorial on Page One The Press declared for Miller for Mayor.

Adam Damm, a fat, jolly, popular man, was ward leader in Ward 23. (The city had just abandoned the proportional representation system and returned to the mayor-ward Council plan.) Damm broke with Miller to support one of his opponents, and Miller invited Lausche to take over direction of his campaign in Ward 23—the Slovenian home ward of the young lawyer.

Lausche was tremendously successful. The ward gave Miller a big vote in the primary and an even

227

bigger one at the election. This was Lausche's first substantial political triumph. He was offered the post of Utilities Director in Miller's Cabinet.

When Lausche told me about the offer, I asked him, "What do you want to do? Where do you want to go in politics?"

"I would like to be a judge," Lausche said.

He declined Miller's offer.

Late in 1932 Miller induced Governor George White to appoint Frank Lausche to the Municipal Court Bench over John L. Mihelich, who was the Democratic boss' personal choice. Miller proposed Lausche on the theory that he could win the election to the unfilled term, which was coming up shortly thereafter, whereas Mihelich could not. He was right.

Lausche received a vote for the Municipal Court Judgeship that startled some of the veteran politicians. His vote-getting ability was to startle them even more in the years to come. It put Frank J. Lausche on a spectacular climb to the Governor's Office.

The young Judge quickly asserted his independence of the political bosses. I learned of one incident after another which revealed his basic integrity. On one occasion, when he would not yield to the demands of an influential politician, reprisal was threatened, but he refused to budge.

Another incident was reported to me by one of the creditors of a small neighborhood bank in which Lausche and some of his friends and relatives were interested. The bank found itself in trouble as a result of the depression, and for almost four years Frank

Lausche used more than half of his Judge's pay to help pay off the bank debts. This meant a real sacrifice for his family, and their home during this period was a small and modest one. That Frank Lausche was not in a strictly legal sense liable for these bank debts made his action the more impressive.

Lausche told me in confidence at about this same time of an incident which shaped his attitude toward politics, in much the same direction that my experiences at the old Police Court had shaped mine. He had been invited over to the office of W. Burr Gongwer, the Democratic political boss, to talk about organizational realignments in that section of Cleveland with which Lausche was most familiar.

The telephone on Gongwer's desk rang. The Democratic boss answered, and it was evident that what he heard irritated him.

"I'll see to that right away, and I'll call you back," Gongwer said. He told his secretary to put in a call for the city's Safety Director.

"I thought you promised me that Smith's place would not be bothered by the police," Gongwer said. "The police are out there right now. This fellow is important to us. He contributed $6,000 to our campaign. I wish you'd get those cops away as soon as you can." Then he reported back to the gambling proprietor, "It's all okeh."

Lausche had not, up to that time, had an opportunity to look in on the higher echelon operations of the political machine. He had worked in Ward 23. He had extended his activity to a large part of the East Side, and had become a fairly substantial leader on the secondary level in organizational politics. Now he had an example of the machine's reciprocal relationships with those who contributed to the organization's treasury. He didn't like it. He determined either to break away from boss-controlled politics or get out of politics altogether.

When The Press first urged Lausche to run for Mayor, in 1935, he decided against it—largely, I believe, for personal reasons. He kept his seat on the Bench. Not long thereafter he again electrified the community by conducting a one-man crusade against gamblers and racketeers who were then corrupting public officials and reaching, in some instances, into our courts.

As the Presiding Judge of Criminal Court, Frank Lausche moved against the most notorious gambling joint in the town, the so-called Harvard Club. He used Assistant County Prosecutors Frank Celebrezze and Anthony J. Rutkowski to carry out his orders. He induced Police Inspector Michael Blackwell to make the raids—and he put the Harvard Club completely out of business in spite of the "home rule" policies of the Sheriff, who declined to interfere with the local authorities of the small village in which the club was located—authorities whom the racketeers were known to control.

When the next election came up, in 1941, Frank J. Lausche was a "natural" for Mayor. The Press again took the upper half of its first page calling upon him to run.

He now decided to abandon his judicial career and make the race for Mayor. He won easily, although by this time—because of his independence of the bosses, his open defiance of them on many occasions, and his fight against the gambling racketeers—the weight of many of the organization's leaders was thrown against him.

Lausche had not been in the Mayor's chair more than a few days when he openly broke with Ray T. Miller, once the hard-hitting Prosecutor and Mayor, who had now become the Democratic boss. The break came over the appointment of the Safety Director, who runs the Police and Fire Department, an important political post. An honest young man named Eliot Ness had been in the post. It was Lausche's aim to retain him. Miller wanted him out.

Lausche refused to remove Ness, and, instead, directed him to clean out every gambling and racketeering place he could locate. Miller never got over it. Through the years the breach between Miller and Lausche has widened, and they are bitter political enemies. Miller has tried to cut Lausche down at every opportunity; he even ran against him for Governor, lining up all the Democratic bosses behind himself for that purpose. But he has never succeeded.

My personal affection and respect for Frank Lausche have increased with the years. His decisions are made regardless of pressures or influences. Many politicians claim they do this, but Lausche actually does it. When he saw politics at work on the lowest and highest levels, he didn't like what he saw, and he has become a kind of political paradox. Most popular political figures are surrounded by a retinue of political characters. Lausche has none. He wants it that way. He likes people, but he wants to be out in public surrounded by them; he abhors being in small and crowded places with those who have axes to grind.

It is clearly understood between us that he is a public figure and I am a newspaper editor; we as a newspaper never hesitated to criticize his actions during the two terms he served as Mayor. He is by nature a suspicious man, but when we were together he relaxed. He knew I wanted nothing from him, and I felt the same way about him.

Lausche attracted state-wide attention by the way he handled his job as Mayor of Cleveland but when it was suggested that he run for Governor, wise politicians scoffed at the idea. The State's conservative political tradition, they thought, would never tolerate for its Governor the son of immigrant Slavs and a Catholic. His close advisers urged against it.

We were together one night, Frank and his wife Jane, Marion and myself.

"What do I do about this Governorship?" he asked.

"Remember the time when the Utilities Directorship had been offered to you?" I asked.

He recalled it.

"I asked you on that occasion two questions, and I am going to repeat them," I said. "The questions were: What do you want to do? Where do you want to go?"

"But they say that the State's tradition is all against me," he said.

"Do you really think that should stop you?" I asked.

"No," Lausche said, "I want to be Governor. I would like to demonstrate, too, that this is really a democracy —that it can be done."

He ran, with every organization leader in the State opposing him. He had no organization of his own. It was necessary to create one from among a few independent people in the eighty-eight counties. His opponents tried to attack him, all over the State, as an "alien" and a Catholic. Groups he had opposed, while Mayor of Cleveland, joined the opposition.

"It's awful rough, Louie," he said in the middle of the campaign. "Awful rough. What they're saying cuts right down into you."

I had learned, as anyone who knows Frank Lausche well has learned, that he has "lost" all his campaigns before election, only to win them on election day. The more discouraged he gets the harder he fights. In this campaign—his first on a state-wide basis—he was discouraged and disillusioned, with no hope of victory. He won by a big vote. This first campaign for the Governorship set the pattern for all others to follow. The bosses, the groups, the blocs were all always against him, but he kept winning, nevertheless.

In 1950, Lausche was faced with a unique question. He admired Senator Robert A. Taft, the man known as "Mr. Republican," who was up for re-election with State Auditor Joe Ferguson running against him. Organized labor threw its might against Taft, and it was a bitter struggle. Lausche as the Democratic Governor of Ohio had to make up his mind either what to do—

or what not to do. He declined to support Ferguson, or to say anything against Taft. This was political heresy, but Lausche stood by his position.

In a small Ohio college town he and Taft sat on the same platform at a commencement. Lausche said some complimentary things about Senator Taft—right squarely in the middle of the campaign—and his remarks raised a storm of protest among Democrats. He refused to retract or modify them in any respect. Taft won by a large margin over Ferguson.

On election day, The Press photographer took a picture of Governor Lausche casting his ballot. The angle at which the picture was taken plainly showed the ballot the Governor was marking, and plainly showed an "X" marked for Senator Taft.

From a newspaper point of view this was a great picture—the picture of Ohio's Democratic Governor voting for "Mr. Republican." It would make Page One in any paper, and it would be sent out by picture services to newspapers all over the country. After some debate in The Press office the picture was shown to me.

The decision was made that The Press had no right to publish the picture, newsworthy as it might be, because it represented a direct invasion of the privacy of an individual—whether a governor or a plain citizen—and of his right to cast his vote in absolute secrecy.

On a "Meet The Press" show Governor Lausche was asked the question: "Did you vote for Senator Taft in the 1950 election?"

He answered that he would be uttering an untruth

if he said that he did not. That answer was no surprise to the staff of The Press, but prior to the Governor's own admission, we had not revealed the information accidentally recorded by the camera.

When Senator Taft died in office, Governor Lausche had to appoint a successor for the unfilled part of Taft's term. He had wanted to be a United States Senator, and he was urged to resign the Governorship after making a deal with the Lieutenant Governor to appoint him to Taft's place.

"If I were to do a thing like that," he told me, "the people would never forgive me, and they would be right. It's dishonest. If I become a Senator, it will only be by election."

He then invited me to accept appointment to the Taft place. I declined, for my life is dedicated to journalism. I quoted to him a statement attributed to Colonel Henry Watterson, the famous Kentucky editor, made under a similar circumstance: "A journalist who a politician would be, never again a journalist can be."

Not long thereafter, he appointed the former Mayor of Cleveland, Thomas A. Burke, who had been Lausche's Director of Law while the Governor had been serving as Cleveland's Mayor. By a very slim margin Congressman George H. Bender defeated Burke's effort to get himself elected to Taft's seat.

Lausche was now serving his fifth term as Governor. He felt, as he expressed himself on the "Meet The Press" television show, in the spring of 1956, that he had no right to ask the people to put him in the Governor's seat a sixth time. He became a candidate for the seat formerly held by his Republican friend and mutual admirer, Senator Bob Taft.

The issue between Bender and Lausche in this campaign centers very largely around what kind of a Democrat Lausche is. The answer is that he isn't a very good Democrat when the capital "D" is used. He is a good democrat with the lower case "d."

"Of course, I believe in the two-party system," Frank Lausche said one evening while we were at dinner. "I believe it is essential to our democracy. That, however, does not mean that I must blindly follow either people or policies I do not believe. It does not require me to take my thinking from political bosses who are in politics for profit, instead of patriotism. If I were ever elected to the United States Senate, I would cross the aisle from one party to the other whenever the interests of the country seemed to require or justify it—regardless."

The Press has campaigned for Lausche each time he has run for Governor. It would like to see him in the United States Senate. That, however, as we understood many years ago when The Press first urged him to run for Mayor of Cleveland, has nothing whatever to do with our complete freedom to oppose him on any issue where we think he is wrong. He was a good Mayor of Cleveland. He is a good Governor of Ohio.

He is, however, not a very good pool player. Whenever I get to Columbus on business we try to get together for a game or two of pool. The Governor's

Mansion is staffed by trusties from the Ohio State Penitentiary—men who in the Warden's opinion have earned a chance to redeem themselves. They are the spectators and they always bet on the Governor.

The game is played as Lausche plays the game of politics—to win. There is something in his nature that, in a contest of any kind, golf, pool, or politics, brings out his determination. He fights vigorously and with intense concentration, but he fights according to rules. When it is over, win or lose, he is gay, relaxed, and funny. It seems almost essential to the Lausche alchemy to be engrossed in some kind of contest, some fight, some challenge.

For the thirty-three-year-old ward leader from the Slovenian National Hall on St. Clair Avenue to become twice Mayor of Cleveland, five times Governor of Ohio, and a national figure in American politics is a triumph for democracy. It is also a triumph for a man who has the capacity for growth—a man who has never stood still in his lifetime, and probably never will. Frank Lausche is a restive, restless, moody, temperamental, fighting, courageous man with the gift of transmitting to other people what he is inside himself. People like and trust him.

He will leave public office a poor man. Jane Lausche has to take care of his money. He won't. She also has to make sure that he looks halfway presentable. He isn't interested in how he looks. Baggy pants, ruffled collar, dirty glasses, rumpled hair neither interest nor bother him. Life is centered for Frank Lausche almost wholly in the mind and spirit. The main passion of his public life is the America to which his parents came. He does not want to let it down, and I don't think he ever will.

Chapter 23

I N A WAY the war years, in spite of the global dispatches that crowded our pages, were the most personalized years of our newspaper. It was evident from the beginning that, since we are the kind of newspaper our tradition makes us, there was a twofold obligation imposed upon us. One of these obligations was, of course, to do everything possible for the servicemen and women—when they were called up, while they were in training, and during their actual service at the front. It was our purpose to follow them straight through from the time they left Cleveland until they returned and, in those tragic instances where they did not return, to do for their families whatever within our power it was possible to do. The other of these obligations was to keep up the spirits and morale of the people at home, and to help keep the community itself moving along in high gear, in both its civic and industrial aspects.

Throughout the war The Press adhered to this program, making a record that would justify putting the paper itself on the "Honor Roll" it created for the men and women of our community.

Even in normal times The Press is unique among the world's newspapers in the number and variety of services it performs for its readers. Some may seem unrelated to the business of publishing a daily newspaper, but all fit into our policy of providing "every possible public service" in addition to complete, accurate, and courageous news reports. The Press Public Service Bureau undertakes many projects merely because they're the neighborly thing to do. Others are large-scale projects which are highly desirable for the entire community, but which might never be undertaken without the leadership and financial support of a daily newspaper. When World War II came upon the country, these services were not only expanded, but almost totally remodeled.

One of the first wartime demands was that for speedy and accurate reporting of the draft lottery results. In most expected situations, such as the draft lottery, The Press operates on the assumption that planning in advance is nine-tenths of the success of the coverage. Planning paid off in this case by making The Cleveland Press the first, by a substantial margin, to get the information, the pictures, the background of the men whose numbers were called.

The Press lost no time in setting up a Military Department which, as was generally acknowledged within our business, was surpassed nowhere. A huge file of photos and facts was assembled on boys in service and where they were assigned. It was thus relatively easy throughout the entire war to follow them in their military exploits. Many newspapers sent their representatives to Cleveland to study our system and adapt it to their own cities.

"The Home Front" was started as a weekly feature. It was a quarter-page digest of the week's news which relatives could clip out—and by the thousands did clip out—and send by V-mail to their servicemen.

"Heir Mail" was another Cleveland Press "first," designed to help morale overseas. Pictures of wives of servicemen with their infants were printed on V-mail blanks so that they could be mailed to their dads, who, in this way, saw their children for the very first time. Many of these pictures were carried by servicemen fathers from almost the beginning to the end of the war.

The Cleveland Press created an "Honor Roll" for all the servicemen and women of the Greater Cleveland area. This was a leather-bound volume, as big as a desktop, illuminated with the American colors and inscribed to the men and women of the service. It was dedicated at a great public meeting held in front of The Cleveland Press building, at which both the Governor and the Mayor signed it as heads of the State and the city. For almost the entire period of the war fathers and mothers, wives and sweethearts made a sacred pilgrimage to the lobby of The Cleveland Press and with their own hands wrote the names of their loved ones, the military units they served in, their date of entering service, and the names of their families. It was necessary to add many volumes to the "Honor Roll" before the war ended. They now repose in the Cleveland Public Library, and many servicemen have gone there to see their names lovingly written in by their relatives.

As the casualties of war began to be returned home, and placed in the big Veterans Hospital named after Cleveland's famous World War I surgeon, Dr. George W. Crile, The Cleveland Press made an appeal to its readers for funds with which to equip the hospital with bedside radios. In a brief and spirited campaign almost $200,000 was raised for this purpose. We arranged with radio people from all over America to join forces in providing what was then considered the best such bedside installation in any American hospital. To this day the approximate one thousand patients at Crile Hospital, veterans of both World War II and Korea, hear music and other entertainment over this radio system. It has a master control station where hundreds of selected records are made available upon the request of the patients.

Many of the best of the world's entertainers, upon coming to Cleveland, have made the trip to Crile to broadcast over the bedside network. Bob Hope and Bing Crosby "took over" there one Sunday afternoon and so completely lost themselves in their entertainment for the veterans that they missed a plane. They never for a moment regretted it.

When the war came to an end, The Cleveland Press set out to raise a large sum of money to finance a suitable memorial in honor of the community's servicemen and women. The Memorial, now being built, is a beautiful fountain within view of the Public Square, situated on Cleveland's Mall, a landscaped stretch between the important public buildings and the lakefront. Around the four corners will be portrayed the basic religions of the world, and at the base will be etched imperishably the name of every Greater Cleveland serviceman and woman killed in World War II and Korea.

One afternoon a young veteran stepped into my office. It was obvious that he was troubled. He fidgeted uneasily with the cap he held in his hands. He had something to say, but he didn't seem to know how to say it, or where to begin. I got up from my desk and went over to sit beside him.

"I don't know what you want to say, Son," I said to him, "but whatever it is why not just let it come out natural?"

It came out—a tragic story that wrenched at my own heart and brought tears to my eyes.

"I just came from the hospital," he said. "My wife has had our first baby. My wife is all right, but when I asked about our baby, I could tell something was wrong by the way the doctor and the nurse acted. They seemed to sort of put me off. Then I told them to let me see my baby—and they took me to the nursery window."

The young veteran began to weep. As I later learned, he was twenty-six; he had a job driving a truck and was very happily married. He told me how he and his wife had dreamed and planned for the arrival of their first-born. They would name him James. They wanted him to be "Jimmy" because the name fit so well their idea of the happy, active boy he would be.

But when the nurse slowly removed the blanket, he saw that his child had no arms from a point below the elbow. One leg was missing from just below the knee, and the other was bent and twisted. When the baby tried to cry he screwed up his face pitifully, and the doctor explained that the baby's tongue was attached to his lower lip.

The young father broke down completely, as he told me how he had gone to his young wife and tried gently to break the news to her—how her heart almost broke for them all—how in her grief she had said at first, "Don't bring him to me. I will not look."

They had no real home. They had only two furnished rooms at a $65 monthly rent which, with medical expenses piling up, was too much for his $50-a-week pay. There was no hospitalization insurance. The world had already crushed in on him. He was desperate.

I talked with the doctor. He told me it was one of the inexplicable paradoxes of birth. Everything had seemed all right, so far as they could tell. There was no injury at birth. Except for the limbs and the mouth, the baby was normal. But there would have to be major surgery and lots of it—some of it uncertain. There would have to be special appliances. There would have to be many months of special care.

If ever there was a heartache baby born to the world this was it—little Jimmy, their first-born, the dream child of the impoverished truckdriver veteran and his young wife. So much needed to be done, and there was so little with which to do it. And the young father and mother wanted the baby with all the fierceness of protective love.

That afternoon I told the young father to go out to the hospital and tell his wife that they would have a home for their son, Jimmy, that there would be doctors, that all he needed would be provided for him. And then we moved into a campaign to raise the required amount of money to provide all this care for Jimmy, to make possible a home outside the city where neighbors wouldn't stare at the tragic little fellow—where the young couple and their son would have a chance.

We started a "Heartache Baby" Fund. Within a few days the fund rose to $12,000. People were helpful in other ways as well: they made land available; they helped to build the house; they volunteered medical and surgical services, needed appliances and household devices. The community showered the "Heartache Baby" with everything but the normal body he didn't have, and had it been within their power to do so, they would gladly have supplied that, too.

Within our memory no appeal so stirred the people of Greater Cleveland as that of the "Heartache Baby" in January of 1949. Jimmy's young parents were beside themselves with gratitude.

"It was not we at The Press," I told them. "We were simply an instrument. We simply told the people of Greater Cleveland the facts about your little son, Jimmy. They did the rest. The people are the ones to thank."

They did thank the people of Greater Cleveland in a statement which they themselves prepared.

"He is ours," the young mother said. "We will take care of him. We thank you for helping us to do that. We will never forget what you have done."

Little Jimmy is now seven. He is a vastly improved little boy. He makes himself understood. He manages to get around. The doctors say that he will over a period of time overcome some of his physical handicaps. He is already a good, fine child, and very bright. His parents have since brought other, normal babies into the world to join Jimmy, and the family is united in a bond of love that the people of Greater Cleveland have helped to forge around the "Heartache Baby."

The Press likes to be that kind of newspaper. It also likes to be a crusading newspaper, fighting constantly for a better Cleveland.

Chapter 24

WHEN AN EDITOR is interviewed, one of the questions likely to be asked is: What is the biggest disaster story of your lifetime as a newspaperman?

I have two answers to this question. One was a disaster that I didn't see. It happened only a year after I became Editor of The Press, when the world-famous Cleveland Clinic was destroyed, claiming several hundred lives, shattering buildings, trapping patients and doctors and nurses and visitors alike in an inevitable death chamber. It was perhaps one of the worst things that has ever happened in America, but that time I only saw the wreckage afterward.

The other I saw with my own eyes. It happened in midafternoon of October 20, 1944. I was to remember that date well. I will remember it for the rest of my life.

I was sitting in my office, chatting with a visitor, when suddenly the building shook as if it had been rocked by an earthquake. There was a sharp, splitting crack, followed by a long, thunderous rumble. My visitor and I looked at each other in surprise. For a moment I thought it might be an explosion in our pressroom, and I started up from my chair to see. As I did so my eyes went to the window.

My office faces east. On bright days I can see an expanse of Lake Erie, with the freighters moving majestically past. On this October afternoon, the sky was reasonably clear, with only a few clouds. But as I looked out of the window, I saw a towering column of black smoke begin to rise over great billows of varicolored smoke. It was located, as nearly as I could guess, several miles to the east somewhere along the lakefront. Even as I watched in fascination there was another great explosion—again shivering our building.

I hurried to the city room. They already had a flash reporting a tremendous explosion, but they didn't know exactly where it was. They knew only that it was in the very heart of a big, residential area off St. Clair Avenue in the general neighborhood of East 55th Street. That would be only a few miles from our office.

It became clear in a few brief moments that this was indeed a disaster. Every piece of equipment available anywhere was dispatched to the scene. Improvised rescue squads were organized and rushed into the area. We too rushed a contingent of reporters out there, and I went along. Over the whole area for miles hung an impenetrable pall of smoke over a raging fire.

Word spreads fast in a disaster. Hundreds of relatives and friends pressed against the police barriers. Nobody was permitted in—for any reason whatever. Only police and firemen could penetrate the great fenced-off territory.

"Stand back, stand back," the order came, repeatedly. "There is danger of another explosion."

Every newspaper reporter is inevitably a witness to tragedy and horror. I had in my time seen a dozen men walk alive into the death chamber at the Ohio Penitentiary and come out dead in wicker baskets after they had been electrocuted in the name of society to pay for their crimes. It was brutal. I almost fainted the first time I saw the executioner throw the switch, saw a man's body jerk convulsively in the dreaded chair, saw the prison physician step forward to examine him with a stethoscope and indicate, perhaps, that another charge of electricity was required. That, I thought at the time, would be the most horrible vision ever to move before my eyes. But it did not match this.

The explosion came—that one, and another, blowing into the already smoke-and-fire-mottled sky houses and buildings and manhole covers and great chunks of other things. The sky must have resembled the catastrophic effects of the blockbuster bombing then going on in other parts of the world, since the end of World War II was at that time still almost a year away.

People stood rooted in horrible fascination and dread. They couldn't speak. They could only look, trying to realize that human beings were trapped out there in that vast, devastated, burning, smoking area, where hundreds of homes lay shattered, where bodies lay unreachable, where human suffering must necessarily be fearful and unbelievable. The explosion ripped and rent and wrecked and burned while firemen heroically strove to get into that cauldron of terror.

I stood shivering—though it was not a cold afternoon and the heat from the wide-burning area blasted incessantly against those of us who were standing there. I shivered from the sheer horror of it all.

Above the firemen's commands, the shouting of police, the cries of relatives, the confusion and chaos, there came the thin cry of a child. It was somewhere nearby. It must be. And yet a sudden concentration of police and firemen in that direction could not track it down. The crowd shuddered in revulsion at the thought of what must be happening to that child whose plaintive call could not be heeded.

Darkness came. The eerie silhouettes of police and firemen, and now (since the restrictions had been lifted) of newspapermen also, including myself, moved through the flickering blazes—a soul-chilling spectacle.

All through the night the fires burned. All through the night ambulances—and hearses—took away the injured and the dead as they were found, twisted or shattered, under the furniture of their homes, under the debris of what they had worked a lifetime to build.

All through the night the homeless were brought to homes and schools and buildings to be tended by the Red Cross and volunteer groups thrown together in common mercy to help the victims.

That night was the worst I have ever experienced. I spent a good part of it in one schoolhouse in particular. My heart was torn apart many times as I talked for hours with parents whose children were gone, or children who would never again see their parents, heard their cries of anguish and watched the valiant effort of both men and women to comfort them, to give them food and clothes, and everything except what they could never again have.

When dawn came, the sun disclosed the ugly, frightening, devastated area. Streets were upheaved. Manhole covers had been catapulted for miles. Buildings were smashed as if they were matchboxes. Daylight showed, too, the rescuers still at their grim work of searching through the ruins for men and women and children known still to be there, and tears came to the eyes of us all.

Like other newspapermen, I went back to my office when morning came, tired, exhausted, emotionally spent, still horrified. I sat down at a typewriter and wrote a short editorial for the first page of our paper. It was addressed to my "Dear Fellow-Townsmen." It was a phrase I had never before used, and I have never used it since. Somehow that day it was the only phrase I felt appropriate. My sense of tragedy and my admiration for the way people had risen to the heights of human heroism and consideration for others was beyond any words. Yet I wrote, as best I could:

> The horror of it so tears a man's heart it is almost impossible for his mind to express his thoughts.
>
> For hours I have walked through the East Area struck by our worst disaster. For a long time in East 55th Street's Willson School I sat with the stunned men, women and children whose homes were destroyed, and whose loved ones are either burned to death, or missing.
>
> It stuns the mind, wrenches the heart.
>
> As we stood before the charred remains of houses and factories, they told me a hundred or more bodies will be dug out in the next few days, to be added to the many already recovered.
>
> Only a few days before I was in this very section, talking for the War Chest, in that very building at 1032 East 62nd Street. A little boy and girl were playing in the street. I found myself praying they were safe.
>
> It is not a tragedy just of lost factories and homes.
>
> We can always replace those.
>
> But the hundreds of men, women and children, homes wiped away, life-long belongings destroyed, all that was precious and dear to them—that's the tragedy.
>
> A greater tragedy is the dead.
>
> The living can be helped—helped by all of us, by our hearts, by our dollars, by our comfort, our community services, our Red Cross, our War Chest, our Civilian Defense. We will do everything possible for those who have suffered more than most of us will ever suffer.
>
> Let all of us, in one mighty expression of our city's collective great heart of compassion, dedicate this week-end to finding out how we may best help those hundreds of our fellow townspeople who so sorely need our help.

A special personal factor added to the unforgettableness of that tragedy for me. On the very day before it happened—at precisely the same hour—I had been standing before a group of people making a talk for the community's War Chest in a building that was now completely blown apart by the blast.

With my realization of my own near escape, something dawned on me. It was an old lesson that often needs to be relearned—the lesson that whatever happens to you at any given time somehow takes on a wholly different importance, no matter how often that same thing has happened to other people. It could happen a million times to a million others, but not until it happens to you do you really appreciate or understand it.

For forty-five years I have been in a business which recounts precisely a variety of personal events and misfortunes—as they have happened to others. I suppose literally hundreds of such news items have passed through my hands.

But, they were "items." I was dealing with them professionally. They had to do, certainly, with people, their homes, their belongings, their happiness, their lives. And, reading them, I was sometimes sympathetic, and sometimes indignant, and sometimes even critical of the people involved. But, after all, they were "items."

It ceases to be an "item" when we ourselves are involved. I can no longer see the report of some human misfortune without somehow sharing with those who have been the victims all the emotions their experience engenders.

I tried to put something of this into an editorial years afterward, in 1953, when by another of life's singularly curious twists my wife was saved from another disaster—this time not by the full day that I was spared, but by only a few moments.

Just before twilight, a tremendous explosion ripped West 117th Street north and south for miles—tearing up pavements, crumpling automobiles like accordions, wrecking buildings and homes—and endangering the lives of all on the street and its nearby tributaries.

It happened at the exact hour of Marion's usual trip home, after her day's work at the Veterans Hospital, over that very street. I realized this the moment I heard of the blast, and my heart twisted within me.

The following morning, I wrote:

Two minutes.

But for this flicker of time today could have been very different for many people—including me.

Like everyone else I have over the years talked with folks who just missed disasters. Who were "almost" on a plane that cracked up. Or were delayed in getting a train that was wrecked. Or were late getting home and were not there when the tornado smashed their place.

Certainly you were relieved to know they escaped harm. It was good to hear. But it really didn't dig down deep into your being as if it had actually happened to you—or yours.

Not until, say, yesterday afternoon, when those two minutes meant everything. When you suddenly realized, as never before in life, what the phrase "narrow escape" from harm—or worse—stands for, what it really can mean.

The lady got into her car outside Crile Hospital. She had finished her day playing the piano, as a Red Cross Gray Lady, for the veterans there.

It is a little before five. She follows mostly the same

route home from Crile, and gets into West 117th somewhat above Lorain.

The sun is shining brightly. It is an ideal autumn afternoon. She stops at a grocery store to pick up a nice ripe cantaloupe. She knows it will please her husband for a late evening snack.

It is now a little after five. She gets back into her car. In a few moments she will be home, 17825 Lake Avenue, where she will meet her husband and they will go out together for the evening.

As her car nears the Berea intersection of West 117th Street, she looks at her watch. It is exactly 5:13. The light turns. She proceeds north toward Lake Avenue.

At Nicholson Avenue and Lake Avenue she hears a tremendous explosion.

Two minutes from Berea and West 117th Street to Nicholson and Lake. Two minutes difference. Two minutes that could have made today a very different day than it is.

Two minutes, also, that bring a greater measure than ever before of understanding and sympathetic regard for others who didn't have that two minutes.

So this morning, as you stand at Berea and West 117th Street at 7:30 with a small group, your thoughts, your understanding, your sympathy for those who were hurt, Mrs. Katherine Szabo, who was killed, her family, and those whose cars were smashed and crushed like tin foil—everything is deeper, and closer, and with much more meaning.

You understand, too, a little better what was meant when a friend said he missed the plane that cracked up, or was late for the train that was wrecked, or didn't get home until after the tornado blew his house to bits.

These things you understand, all the better, because of those two minutes—the two minutes which could have made today a very different day than it is.

I wish that God had granted those two minutes to all.

Chapter 25

I HEAR many things said about me, or hear reports of things said, that are anything but complimentary. I am aware that in the heat of campaigns my name is kicked about on the public platform. It is to be expected. It is part of my business. It is the inevitable consequence of being connected with a fighting newspaper. People would not be human, if they did not fight back in their own way.

An example is the election of Anthony J. Celebrezze.

Tony Celebrezze is the current Mayor of Cleveland. His political experience, until he first ran for office himself in 1950, was confined to working with his brother, the late Frank D. Celebrezze. Frank had been an Assistant County Prosecutor, had been briefly in the thirties a Municipal Judge, and later was Safety Director in the cabinets of Lausche and Burke.

Somebody Is Getting Away With Murder

AN EDITORIAL

What's the matter with the law enforcement authorities of Cuyahoga County?

Have they lost their sense of reason?—or at least inexcusably set aside the realization of what they are hired to do, and for whom they work?

If ever a murder case was studded with fumbling, halting, stupid, uncooperative bungling—politeness to people whose place in this situation completely justified vigorous searching, prompt and effective police work—the Sheppard case has them all.

Was the murder of Mrs. Sheppard a polite matter? Did the killer make a dutiful bow to the authorities and then proceed brutally to destroy the young child-bearing wife?

Why all of this sham, hypocrisy, politeness, criss-crossing of pomp and protocol in this case?

Who is trying to deceive whom?

•

From the very beginning of this case—from the first hour that the murder became known to the authorities by a telephone call from the husband to the town mayor—from that moment on and including this, the case has been one of the worst in local crime history.

Of course the trail is cold. Of course the clews have been virtually erased by the killer. Of course the whole thing is botched up so badly that head or tail cannot be made of it.

In the background of this case are friendships, relationships, hired lawyers, a husband who ought to have been subjected instantly to the same third-degree to which any other person under similar circumstances is subjected, and a whole string of special and bewildering extra-privileged courtesies that should never be extended by authorities investigating a murder—the most serious, and sickening crime of all.

The spectacle of a whole community watching a batch of law enforcement officials fumbling around, stumbling over one another, bowing and scraping in the presence of people they ought to be dealing with just as firmly as any other persons in any other crime—that spectacle is not only becoming a stench but a serious threat to the dignity of law enforcement itself.

•

Coroner Sam Gerber was never more right than when yesterday he said that the killer must be laughing secretly at the whole spectacle—the spectacle of a community of a million and a half people brought to indignant frustration by Mrs. Sheppard's killer in that white house out in Bay Village.

Why shouldn't he chuckle? Why shouldn't he cover up, shut up, conceal himself behind the circle of protecting people?

What's the matter with us in Cuyahoga County? Who are we afraid of? Why do we have to kow-tow to a set of circumstances and people where a murder has been committed?

•

It's time that somebody smashed into this situation and tore aside this restraining curtain of sham, politeness and hypocrisy and went at the business of solving a murder—and quit this nonsense of artificial politeness that has not been extended to any other murder case in generations.

Why No Inquest? Do It Now, Dr. Gerber

AN EDITORIAL

Why hasn't County Coroner Sam Gerber called an inquest into the Sheppard

And—what's most important of all—it sometimes solves crimes.

What good reason is there now for

Why Don't the Police Quiz No. 1 Suspect?

AN EDITORIAL

You can bet your last dollar the Sheppard murder would be cleaned up long ago if it had involved "average people."

They'd have hauled in all the suspects to Police Headquarters.

grill him at Police Headquarters, like the chief suspect in any murder case.

But they didn't.

And they haven't.

In fairness, they've made some progress.

Quit Stalling and Bring Him In!

(AN EDITORIAL)

[illegible]

But the people of Cuyahoga County expect you, the law enforcement officials, to protect the people's rights.

A murder has been committed. You know who the chief suspect is.

[illegible]

What the people of Cuyahoga County cannot understand, and The Press cannot understand, is why you are showing Sam Sheppard so much more consideration as a murder suspect than any other person who has ever before been suspected in a murder case.

Why?

CELEBREZZE SAYS BAY MAYOR IS PROTECTING MURDER SUSPECT

Louis B. Seltzer and Governor Frank J. Lausche
at Miami University (Ohio), when the Editor was
made an honorary LL.D. (1956)

PHOTO BY JAMES THOMAS

The Louis B. Seltzers and their grandchildren,
Ted and Leigh Cooper (1956)

One day I was walking on a downtown street toward my office when a small, thin, intense-eyed man stopped me. This was the older of the brothers, Frank. Many times he and I had fought over issues, but we had never fought over this man's basic honesty or independence. He was one of the most honorable men in the city.

That day Frank had something on his mind. He wanted to call my attention to his young brother Tony, who was making himself a student of government and was ambitious for public office. "Tony is growing fast," Frank said proudly. "He's independent. One of these days I would like to see him sit in the Mayor's chair. He would make a good Mayor."

Tony Celebrezze is an immigrant Italian whose father, after living some years in America, had taken his family back to Italy. Later, when Tony was still a babe, they returned to Cleveland.

Tony worked at odd jobs—as newsboy, freight handler, anything he could get—to pay his way through school. He passed the bar examination in 1936, and then got his first public appointment. He was hired to do legal work for the Ohio Unemployment Commission.

Tony stepped out on his own in 1950 as a candidate for State Senator at the Democratic primaries. With little support, he was nominated and elected. In the Ohio Senate, where Democrats were few, he stood out conspicuously. He had a flair for oratory—and when he took the floor he attracted attention. He became popular with the Republican majority, and formed strong friendships there. In this session Frank J. Lausche, the independent-minded Governor of Ohio, was not always seeing eye to eye with the Democratic floor leader, and he often leaned heavily on Tony Celebrezze to help him carry out his program. Celebrezze was regarded in some quarters as the unofficial spokesman for the Governor—although, on some issues he differed vigorously with the Executive.

At the conclusion of the session, Celebrezze was rated among the four top men in the Senate, and top among the Democrats—an unusual situation for a young first-termer.

At that point Tony Celebrezze's "troubles" began, because he insisted upon following his own conscience. This was what attracted The Cleveland Press to him.

In 1952, he sought renomination. He engaged in a running fight with Ray T. Miller, the Democratic chief, because he chose to support Michael DiSalle for U.S. Senator over James M. Carney, the choice of the Miller organization. Tony was chastised by the organization for this defection; nevertheless, he carried the election, leading the ticket in the primaries and proving an easy winner in November.

In the 1953 session, Celebrezze and the Democratic floor leader were at war frequently—and his break with the organization was wide open.

Tom Burke decided not to run for another term as Mayor of Cleveland. The Democratic organization quickly drafted County Engineer Albert S. Porter as its candidate, while the Republicans got behind William J. McDermott, Juvenile Court Judge, who had resigned to enter the race and was regarded as the favorite to win.

I remembered Frank Celebrezze's remark to me about his younger brother, Tony—and recalled, too, how courageously Tony had handled himself in the Legislature. That afternoon, after talking to him, I sat down and wrote an editorial for Page One vigorously endorsing Tony Celebrezze for Mayor as an independent—as a man completely free from boss control, controlled only by his own conscience.

Tony took the paper out to the hospital where Frank, whom he worshiped, was now gravely ill, and read the editorial aloud to him. I've always been glad Frank knew about that editorial. Three hours later he died.

The other two newspapers in Cleveland were divided in their endorsements—The News for McDermott, The Plain Dealer for Porter. Retiring Mayor Tom Burke, who had sat in on the meetings drafting Porter, kept neutral in the campaign. Lausche campaigned for Celebrezze, praising him for his work in the Legislature.

This was a run-off primary with the first two winners confronting each other at the regular November election. It was generally assumed that McDermott would come out first, Porter second, and Celebrezze third. Celebrezze won by a substantial margin, topping McDermott with Porter third. In the November election Celebrezze beat McDermott decisively.

It is true that The Press had actively supported

Celebrezze, and might thus have had something to do with his decisive victory. But some people started to call Tony Celebrezze "Louie's Mayor"—saying that he took his instructions from "Ninth and Rockwell," where The Press building is located. They talked, knowingly, about a "private wire" between The Press and City Hall.

There was no truth in that.

Grandpa Lucien Bonaparte used to have a good many wise sayings which I have remembered all my life, and one of them came in handy now: "Don't ever be concerned about anything people say about you, unless it's true."

It is now almost forty-five years that I have been in a business where there is continual controversy—where there are almost always two sides to every story—where vigorous positions on both people and questions are taken—where crusades are launched and battles fought —where it is sometimes necessary to condemn people as well as to praise them.

It is inevitable that from it all there is distilled toward an editor some ill feeling—some doubts and suspicions—some charges of arrogance and thirst for power —some notions about bossism and political maneuvering.

William Allen White warned me against this many years ago.

"There will be times, Louie," he said, "when you wish you'd pulled up stakes and left your home town. It's a penalty we have to pay in our business. When we do something people like we are cheered. When we do something they don't like, they forget what they cheered about and jeer—and sometimes, the jeers sound louder in your ears than the cheers. You have to go on doing the very best you can, and hope that in the end what you are, the motives which prompted you, the fairness by which you appraised things, will come out, and that people will get to know you so well they'll just take you for what you are. If you can get to that place with the people in your home town, that's about all you have a right to expect."

The mixture of equal parts of William Allen White and Grandpa Lucien Bonaparte Seltzer—together with whatever I have learned about the people in my home city of Cleveland—has been an elixir that stimulated me sufficiently to withstand some bad moments. Fortunately, they have been relatively few.

I provided another spectacular example of how and why a newspaper editor gets the "political boss" tag fastened on him in the election of November, 1955, involving a young Cleveland lawyer named Tom Parrino. The chances are that Tom Parrino spent less to get himself elected a judge in a big city than anybody in modern political history. It cost him less than $50.

The Cleveland Press had been watching Parrino for quite a while. He was able, vigorous, courageous, and independent—qualities which we, as a newspaper, like in public officials.

Tom is a native Clevelander, although the son of Italian immigrants, like Tony Celebrezze, the Mayor. By an interesting coincidence he worked his way through the same school where Celebrezze struggled to graduation as an honor student—Ohio Northern University. Tom passed the bar examination in 1942 and promptly went into the Army, even before he had time to hang out his shingle. He came out of the service in 1946. That is only ten years ago, but in that decade Tom Parrino came up in public esteem—and in the esteem of The Press—like a self-guided projectile.

For nearly five years Parrino was at the trial table in nearly every big case tried in the criminal courts around Cleveland. He came to be one of the best trial lawyers in the Prosecutor's Office.

His big break came in the sensational Sheppard trial in 1954. Parrino was one of the trio of prosecutors who carried the case for the State versus Sam Sheppard. His deft handling of witnesses, the skill he displayed in the courtroom, the thoroughness with which he had prepared evidence introduced by the prosecution brought him to the attention of the whole Cleveland Bench and Bar—and to the specific attention of one of Cleveland's largest and most successful law firms, Squires, Sanders and Dempsey. The firm was looking for a trial lawyer —and in June, 1955, offered Parrino a job. He accepted the appointment and left the Prosecutor's Office.

He had for practical purposes put public office behind him forever. "Forever" wasn't very long.

In the fall of 1955, David C. Meck, an incumbent judge, died suddenly. At the time of his death he was up for re-election, and had been unopposed. It was held that there was no time to replace him on the ballot. It was also ruled that his place could only be filled by a write-in vote at the November election. A great many lawyers entered the write-in campaign. Bernard Conway, the Chief City Police Prosecutor who had the support of the Bar Associations and the other two Cleveland newspapers, was the favorite in the list.

The Press heard that Parrino might be receptive to the idea of running for the write-in election. He was by far the ablest of any who had either announced, or been considered. The Press moved in quickly and persuaded Parrino to make up his mind.

By this time the election was only one week away. The other candidates had a considerable head start, and at first the experts scoffed at the idea that Parrino had a chance. Toward the end of the election it began to look as if that picture had changed.

Because of the shortness of time before the election, The Press had to hit hard and often. Even more important, we devised some exceedingly simple suggestions on how to write in the name, making use of diagrams and sample ballots to clarify the procedure.

The Bar Associations, while admiring Parrino himself, felt that his campaign broke into their own slate of candidates, as, of course, it did. Usually, all things being equal, The Press would so far as possible go along with the Bar's recommendations, since they canvass the field thoroughly. Nevertheless, as in other instances of the past, we believed Parrino to be so exceptionally well qualified for the Bench that we were willing to risk incurring the Bar Associations' displeasure.

Parrino won. He won big, leading by more than two to one over the nearest man on the list, the generally supported Bernard Conway.

As was true of Mayor Celebrezze, some of the town's livelier conversationalists tagged Tom Parrino as one of "The Press Boys"—as one of "Louie's Stable." Most of the people of Cleveland recognized our support of Parrino for what it was—and is—a newspaper's honest judgment about good men in public office. This is where democracy is made or broken—and this is where a newspaper's obligation clearly rests, if it is genuinely concerned about the security, stability, and safety of the community which sustains it in business.

The Press is the first to take issue with, fight against, or otherwise disagree with any person, including those it may have sponsored or vigorously fought for in an election campaign. We assume no obligation, extend no blank check to anyone. The public acts of an official we've helped elect are scrutinized, by our editorial "eye," in exactly the same way as those of an official we have opposed for office. We recognize only one obligation—our obligation to the public which reposes its confidence in our newspaper. For that confidence the least we can do in return for people is to fight eternally in their interests, with courage, vision, vigor, and forthrightness.

I have a simple philosophy by which my whole newspaper life has been guided—especially as Editor of The Cleveland Press. It is that whatever is in the ultimate best interest of the community is selfishly in the best interest of The Press. It is up to us to help the community grow and prosper, to fight those things which are harmful to it and to fight with equal vigor for those things we believe will make the community a better place in which to live.

I have one more basic principle, one that has enabled me to go through many hard-slugging political campaigns with few scars. Not by so much as lifting an eyebrow, not by telephone, by letter, or in any other way, have we ever sought to obtain any favor, any job, any privilege, from anybody in public life, no matter how trivial, or for whatever purpose. We will not confer with anyone other than in the columns of our newspaper about any matter having to do with either government or politics. We are a newspaper, wholly and exclusively—and in no way concerned with or interested in political tactics, strategies, or groups. We are either Republican or Democratic depending upon the fitness of the candidates for a given office. We are independent of any party, group, or special interest of any kind whatever. We are free to make our own choices, take our own position, fight for or against whatever we think is right or wrong.

Even in local matters, there is sometimes a penalty attached to taking a stand. For example, I live in a suburban neighborhood, on the near side of a valley with a narrow bridge over it. The phenomenal growth of our metropolitan community has resulted in serious traffic congestion there. The only solution is to build a new bridge. It is proposed that the approach be routed through the neighborhood in which we live, cutting straight through some of my neighbors' property and, in fact, right at the back line of my own.

The Press favors this proposed bridge route as being essential to the best interest of the greatest number. My neighbors are incensed, because they believe that I have betrayed them. I understand exactly how they feel. In fact, if somebody else were editing a newspaper that favored a through route on the back line of my property, I would feel the same way. But I cannot betray my own trust as a newspaper editor.

Early in our business we have to make up our minds to take the bumps and bruises that come our way. We live in a business where we give; by the same token we must learn to take.

Chapter 26

O N THE MORNING of July 4, 1954, Mrs. Marilyn Reese Sheppard, a pretty Bay Village housewife, was found bludgeoned to death in her bedroom.

For mystery, for suspense, for painstaking putting together of fragmentary clews by the most scientific methods, the Sheppard murder, which was to become one of the country's most famous in modern times, had within it all of the elements of the classic criminal case.

It had one other element, which set it apart from most murder cases of this type. That was the deliberate effort to prevent the law enforcement authorities from finding the killer. The case became both a murder and, in a very real sense, a roadblock against the law.

At the time Marilyn Reese Sheppard was brutally

killed, only two other persons were present in the quiet lakefront home, settled among big trees a comfortable distance away from the roadway. One of these was Dr. Samuel H. Sheppard, her husband, a young, handsome, athletic osteopath, and, the other, the Sheppards' sleeping son Chip, aged six.

Bay Village is a tightly knit community to the west of Cleveland. It is composed largely of young people who either have their own businesses, are fairly well established in the professions, or have a competence. It is a community of beautiful homes, peaceful and quiet, but socially vivacious. Families visit back and forth in the easy, relaxed, and buoyant way common to newly created small communities with a youthful flavor. They are very loyal to one another when any form of trouble occurs.

The family of Dr. Sam Sheppard owned a large osteopathic hospital in the village. His father and brothers operated it, with Sam Sheppard, of course, also on the staff.

It was to the Sheppard family's hospital that Dr. Sam was taken by his family immediately after the murder of his wife was reported. The reason given for hospitalizing him was that an intruder—a bushy-haired man, as Dr. Sam described him—had injured his neck in the struggle the Doctor reported had taken place in the house. Thus, the Sheppard family surrounded Dr. Sam.

The investigating authorities were blocked off. The Mayor of Bay Village was J. Spencer Houk, who owned the local butcher shop and was a close friend of Dr.

Sam. They visited back and forth; they went on vacations together; they owned a boat together. Mayor Houk rejected the advice of Coroner Sam Gerber and the Cleveland Homicide Squad that Dr. Sam should be arrested.

Dr. Sam was fenced in by his family, his friends, and the public authorities in Bay Village. The protective wall had been put up quickly. It was almost impossible to penetrate it, and then only at the will of those who controlled the encirclement—and on their terms. The purpose seemed obvious—to hold the wall secure around Dr. Sam until public interest subsided, and the investigating authorities turned their attention elsewhere.

The newspapers began to lose interest—except one. The Press kept the Sheppard murder case in top position on Page One. It kept steadily prying into the case, asking questions, trying to break through the wall around Dr. Sam.

On July 15, eleven days after Marilyn Reese Sheppard's badly beaten body had been found in the bedroom of their home, I addressed a list of eleven questions to Dr. Sam and his lawyers—one of whom was a prominent criminal lawyer hired by the Sheppard family the very morning Marilyn's body had been found.

Dr. Sam's reply was published on July 17. The answers were noninformative and inconclusive. The situation was just as tight, just as completely road-blocked, just as walled in as before.

On July 20, with the investigation lagging, with the

Coroner still fended off by the family and Bay Village friends and officials, The Press published on Page One an editorial. It took the upper quarter of the page, and the eight-column heading said: "Somebody Is Getting Away With Murder."

It was a calculated risk—a hazard of the kind which I believed a newspaper sometimes in the interest of law and order and the community's ultimate safety must take. I was convinced that a conspiracy existed to defeat the ends of justice, and that it would affect adversely the whole law-enforcement machinery of the County if it were permitted to succeed. It could establish a precedent that would destroy even-handed administration of justice.

Because I did not want anyone else on The Press staff to take the risk, I wrote the editorial myself. It may not have been a good editorial, but it was a hard-hitting editorial. It was intended to be. It read in part:

> What's the matter with the law enforcement authorities of Cuyahoga County?
> Have they lost their sense of reason?—or, at least inexcusably, set aside the realization of what they are hired to do, and for whom they work?
> If ever a murder case was studded with fumbling, halting, stupid, incooperative bungling—politeness to people whose place in this situation completely justified vigorous searching, prompt and effective police work—the Sheppard case has them all.
> Was the murder of Mrs. Sheppard a polite matter?
> Did the killer make a dutiful bow to the authorities and, then, proceed brutally to destroy the young child-bearing wife?
> Why all of this sham, hypocrisy, politeness, crisscrossing of pomp and protocol in this case?

Who is trying to deceive whom?

From the very beginning—from the first hour that the murder became known to the authorities by a telephone call from the husband to the Town Mayor—from that moment on, and including this, the case has been one of the worst in local crime history.

Of course, the trail is cold. Of course, the clews have been virtually erased by the killer. Of course, the whole thing is botched-up so badly that head or tail cannot be made of it.

In the background of this case are friendships, relationships, hired lawyers, a husband who ought to have been subjected instantly, to the same third-degree to which any other person, under similar circumstances, is subjected, and a whole string of special and bewildering extra-privileged courtesies that should never be extended by authorities investigating a murder—the most serious and sickening crime of all.

The spectacle of a whole community watching a batch of law enforcement officials fumbling around, stumbling over one another, bowing and scraping in the presence of people they ought to be dealing with just as firmly as any other persons in any other crime—that spectacle is not only becoming a stench, but a serious threat to the dignity of law enforcement itself.

Coroner Sam Gerber was never more right than when yesterday he said that the killer must be laughing secretly at the whole spectacle—the spectacle of a community of a million and a half people brought to indignant frustration by Mrs. Sheppard's killer in that white house out in Bay Village.

Why shouldn't he chuckle? Why shouldn't he cover up, shut up, conceal himself behind the circle of protecting people?

What's the matter with us in Cuyahoga County? Who are we afraid of? Why do we have to kow-tow to a set of circumstances and people where a murder has been committed?

It's time that somebody smashed into this situation

and tore aside this restraining curtain of sham, politeness, and hypocrisy, and went at the business of solving a murder—and quit this nonsense of artificial politeness that has not been extended to any other murder case in generations.

The evening this editorial was published in The Press on Page One, the Bay Village City Council met and voted to take the investigation away from their own police force and hand it over to the Cleveland Police Department's Homicide Squad.

The next day, also on Page One, The Press published an editorial headed: "Why No Inquest? Do It Now, Dr. Gerber."

> Why hasn't County Coroner Sam Gerber called an inquest into the Sheppard murder case?
> What restrains him?
> Is the Sheppard case any different from the countless other murder mysteries where the Coroner has turned to this traditional method of investigation?
> An inquest empowers use of subpoena.
> It puts witnesses under oath.
> It makes possible the examination of every possible witness, suspect, relative, record and papers available anywhere.
> It puts the investigation itself into the record.
> And—what's most important of all—sometimes solves crimes.
> What good reason is there now for Dr. Gerber to delay any longer the use of the inquest?
> The murder of Marilyn Sheppard is a baffling crime.
> Thus far, it appears to have stumped everybody.
> It may never be solved.
> But this community can never have a clear conscience, until every possible method is applied to its solution.

What, Coroner Gerber, is the answer to the question—

Why don't you call an inquest into this murder?

A few hours after this editorial appeared on Page One of The Cleveland Press, Coroner Gerber ordered an inquest.

At the inquest, Dr. Sam insisted his married life had been a happy one. He denied an "affair" with a former Bay Village Hospital technician now living in California. The Press flew a reporter to Los Angeles with the police. The technician was brought back to Cleveland. She admitted her affair with Dr. Sam, and related talks she had with Dr. Sam about a possible marriage.

The wall still surrounded Dr. Sam. He had gone back to the family-operated hospital.

On July 30, The Cleveland Press published, again spread across the top of its first page, another editorial. This one was headed: "Quit Stalling—Bring Him In." Once more I wrote it myself. It was my neck I was sticking out.

> Maybe somebody in this town can remember a parallel for it. The Press can't.
> And not even the oldest police veterans can, either.
> Everybody's agreed that Sam Sheppard is the most unusual murder suspect ever seen around these parts.
> Except for some superficial questioning during Coroner Sam Gerber's inquest, he has been scot-free of any official grilling into the circumstances of his wife's murder.
> From the morning of July 4, when he reported his wife's killing, to this moment, 26 days later, Sam Sheppard has not set foot in a police station.
> He has been surrounded by an iron curtain of pro-

tection that makes Malenkov's Russian concealment amateurish.

His family, his Bay Village friends—which include its officials—his lawyers, his hospital staff, have combined to make law enforcement in this County look silly.

The longer they can stall bringing Sam Sheppard to the police station the more surer it is he'll never get there.

The longer they can string this whole affair out the surer it is that the public's attention sooner, or later, will be diverted to something else, and then the heat will be off, the public interest gone, and the goose will hang high.

This man is a suspect in his wife's murder. Nobody yet has found a solitary trace of the presence of anybody else in the Lake Road house the night or morning his wife was brutally beaten to death in her bedroom.

And yet, no murder suspect in the history of this County has been treated so tenderly, with such infinite solicitude for his emotions, with such fear of upsetting the young man.

Gentlemen of Bay Village, Cuyahoga County, and Cleveland, charged jointly with law enforcement—

This is murder. This is no parlor game. This is no time to permit anybody—no matter who he is—to outwit, stall, fake, or improvise devices to keep away from the police or from the questioning anybody in his right mind knows a murder suspect should be subjected to— at a police station.

The officials throw up their hands in horror at the thought of bringing Sam Sheppard to a police questioning for grilling. Why? Why is he any different than anybody else in any other murder case?

Why should the police officials be afraid of Bill Corrigan, his lawyer? Or anybody else, for that matter, when they are at their sworn business of solving a murder?

Certainly, Corrigan will act to protect Sam Sheppard's rights. He should.

But the people of Cuyahoga County expect you, the law enforcement officials, to protect the people's rights.

A murder has been committed. You know who the chief suspect is.

You have the obligation to question him—question him thoroughly and searchingly—from beginning to end, and not at his hospital, not at his home, not in some secluded spot out in the country.

But at Police Headquarters—just as you do every other person suspected in a murder case.

What the people of Cuyahoga County cannot understand, and The Press cannot understand, is why you are showing Sam Sheppard so much more consideration as a murder suspect than any other person who has ever before been suspected in a murder case.

Why?

That night Dr. Sam was arrested on a murder charge and taken to Police Headquarters.

The rest of the Sam Sheppard case is familiar. He was indicted by the Grand Jury, tried in a courtroom crowded with newspaper, radio, and television representatives from all over America, convicted of second degree murder, and sentenced to the Ohio Penitentiary, where he is now a prisoner.

The Cleveland Press was both applauded and criticized. It was criticized on the ground that The Press inflamed public opinion by its persistent and vigorous pounding away at the case. It was criticized by some who expressed the belief that the Sheppard case had been "tried" in the newspapers before it reached the courtroom.

The question confronting The Press, as a newspaper properly concerned about the whole structure of law enforcement in the community, was—

Shall we permit a protective wall to shield a solution to this murder, by saying and doing nothing, or—

Shall we move in with all of our editorial artillery in an effort to bring the wall down, and make it possible for law enforcement authorities to act in their normal and accustomed way?

There were risks both ways. One represented a risk to the community. The other was a risk to The Press. We chose the risk to ourselves.

As Editor of The Press I would do the same thing over again under the same circumstances.

Chapter 27

A S I LOOK BACK on the exciting years that
newspaper work have given me, and look
forward to the equally exciting years ahead,
I feel deeply sad that my father could not have shared
more of these years with me. I suppose I should be glad
that he was able to share so many of them. But as I sat
before the typewriter in my office on the morning of
February 10, 1942, I discovered that it was hard to write
through tears. What I wanted to write was my farewell
to the man who had been my hero from boyhood. But
the tears got in my way.

Somehow I just sat there, remembering. I remembered what my Dad meant to me—the things he did for
me—the example he set for me—the truly great influence he had exerted upon my life. It had been a

rare privilege to be his son, to inherit some of the extraordinary stuff of which he was made, to experience the mutual love and respect we had held for each other from the time I was old enough to think until the few hours ago when he left us.

That morning I thought about many things, and across the screen of my mind and heart I saw a virtually unending procession of wonderful images of him.

Success came to my father in a big way after a long hardship in his earlier years. It did not spoil him. It did not even change him. More than any other man he remained constant and true to his inner convictions and natural self.

"The big thing in life," he frequently told us as children, "is to take everything in stride—the good and the bad, happiness and sorrow, the ups and the downs. It is an old saying but a good one, 'The higher you are —the harder you fall.' When you are on the way up, always remember that you may be seeing the same people on the way down, so be sure you never forget them, or they may forget you."

Sometimes fathers and sons tend to separate. Sons grow up. Fathers grow old. Sons marry, have their own homes, their own families, their own interests. Even when they live only a few blocks apart, this separation often takes place. It is a tragedy that this is so.

Between Father and myself, and his other two sons, there was fortunately no such separation when we grew up—or even in the process of growing up. We were drawn even closer.

I was both the oldest and the smallest of his three

sons. My father was six foot two in his bare feet. He was a powerfully built man. When he was in his prime he liked to test his strength at the machines they used to have at the circus or on the fair ground. He could send the ball almost to the top by the impact of a hammer's blow. He got a lot of pleasure from smacking it hard, and seeing it go.

I was the runt of the family. In my bare feet I could hardly make it to five foot six. As a child, if there was any contagious disease floating around the neighborhood, I was the one who picked it up.

Because I was slight and frail Father tended to gather me to him psychologically. We sensed a mutuality of concern. He never forgot the decision I made to go out after a job when the family was hard up, and he tried ever afterward in one way or another to make it up to me.

"You were such a little tike when you did that," he would say many times later, and pat me on the back. "I didn't think you had it in you. But, by gosh, you did."

He liked to have a little fun at my expense too. When I came into the world, Father and Mother were living in a two-room affair behind a fire engine house on Clark Avenue, on the West Side of Cleveland. They had to stave off the creditors, and borrow money for the doctor.

"We debated whether to keep you, or trade you in for a loaf of bread," he used to tell me.

I remembered the time, when he had hit his literary stride and money was coming in at a pretty good rate, that he took me aside, saying, "Son, I think you better go back to school."

But he was not displeased even when I would not agree to go. "If that's the way you want it, let's keep it that way," he said. "If we can't be honest with each other then we can't respect or love each other, can we?"

He seemed always to keep his feet squarely fixed on earth whenever he talked with us. Always he stressed assuming responsibility, always he urged us to make our own decisions, to be decisive, to know what we wanted to do and have the courage and the "get-up," as he described it, to do it.

By the time I married and left home, Father was writing books and stories at a prodigious rate. The publishers were really coming after him for his novels now. There was competition. He moved to a better house in a suburb, and they came out to his home from New York and elsewhere to see him. Robert H. Davis of Munsey's became a special friend of Father's. They liked the same things and even resembled each other in many ways.

Bob Davis brought Father and Irvin Cobb together. Once they went down to Cobb's birthplace in Paducah, Kentucky, to fish. Father came back and made our house rock with laughter when he told how Irvin Cobb flopped into a stream, when a fish he described as a "minnow" pulled him in head over heels. Cobb was a man of vast physical proportions, and Father's graphic account of the incident made one of the best stories he ever told—particularly when he portrayed portly Irvin

Cobb, cigar still stuck at a belligerent angle, dispatching the fish to the piscatorial counterpart of Hell.

Other interesting personalities began to appear at Father's home. Harry Carey, one of Hollywood's most popular Western actors, was a visitor every time he came East. Father and Harry Carey would do a lot of reminiscing about the West, and some of their stories reminded me of those told in the early days by Nick Roth. They got a great kick out of our intense concentration on what they said, and their own exchange of reassurance:

"Wasn't that right, Harry?" Or, "We sure did, didn't we, Charley?"

William S. Hart, tall, gaunt, taciturn, who blazed two guns in the movies from both hips simultaneously, was one of Father's favorite actors. He was particularly happy when Bill Hart was billed in the leading role of one of his books.

Once when Bill Hart came to Cleveland and almost the whole town turned out to see him, he sought out Father.

"I liked playing in that story of yours, Charley," Bill Hart said, and Father was in high spirits for weeks afterward, especially when one of the papers printed the remark.

Zane Grey and Father were contemporaries, and also friends. They both wrote Westerns. They were both Ohioans. They were both prolific writers. In a sense they conceived themselves to be friendly competitors, and they corresponded often.

"Why didn't you start writing before or after I did?" Father wrote to Zane Grey one time.

"If I had started before, you wouldn't have had anything left to write," Zane Grey retorted. "And if I had waited until after you got finished I'd have passed out from literary thirst in the middle of an idea desert. So it's a stand-off. Let's keep it the way it is. By the way, what's the plot of your next story so I can avoid duplicating it in my next one?"

There was quite a bit of good-natured ribbing between them on how much each actually knew about the "Old West" for which they appeared to be the current fictional historians. My father yielded to Zane Grey in actual residence in the West, but tripped him up periodically on some of his descriptions and the identification of its denizens and landmarks.

"I think I can spell you down, Zane, in a contest on which of us knows most about what we're writing about," Father wrote to Zane Grey on one occasion.

"When will it be, Charley, and at how many paces from the realities?" Grey wrote back.

There was a period when books by Zane Grey and Father were actually published almost simultaneously, and on the bookstands of America they were advertised together. On one occasion in particular they came out the same week and were reviewed at the same time.

Father wrote a note to Zane Grey, saying, "Let's arrange our idea timetables a bit."

Zane Grey wrote back:

"All right, Charley, I'm dry for a while—the spring is exhausted for the time being—it'll be some time before it refreshes itself with another idea. It's your turn."

Father admired Zane Grey, not only as an expert craftsman in the field, but for his vivid and dramatic technique. It was quite obvious that Zane Grey likewise held a high regard for Father.

Nothing pleased Father more than to have his whole family around him. He invented every reason possible to bring us together, and Mother always took special delight in preparing the meals for us. She baked bread, made cookies, fixed cakes with deep frosting, and had several varieties of almost everything. We always suspected that it was their way of saying that they knew the family larder was not always abundant when we were children, and that now they wanted to make sure we shared in their good fortune.

How much our lives centered, I often thought, around Father and Mother. They represented the refuge, the sanctuary, the anchor for us. Many times, as I grew older, my heart went out to the children in homes broken apart by divorce, or filled with heartaches and misery.

Father and Mother had their share of differences, but they were never serious. We never regarded their quarrels as important, for we knew they would not last.

Discipline was accepted in our home. There were rules, made to be respected. Any breach of them brought some kind of punishment. Father's razor strop, which hung behind our kitchen door, was not always used for its original purpose. It found its stinging way across our "sitters" whenever the judgment of our parents felt it was essential to the preservation of household order. So far as I could tell this punishment didn't induce any of the inferiority which modern child psychologists dread. It did induce respect for our parents and appreciation for the rules of the game, or the home, or the community, or society.

Father had strong opinions about the home, about marriage, about children. He expressed them frequently, both in private and, later, in speeches and interviews. On one occasion he said:

> Parents themselves should be strong if they expect their children to be strong. I don't believe parents should try to dominate their children. They have no right to do so. They bring their children into the world because they want them. They should love their children, and they should respect them as individual personalities just as they hope children will in turn respect their parents as personalities.
>
> Everything should be done to make a home good, wholesome, sound, orderly, with specific understandings of how it should be run, and the place of every one in it. Everyone in a home should have a certain responsibility for it, including children, from the moment they are capable of understanding. They should be gradually influenced to assume responsibility, make their own decisions, build their own personalities.
>
> Parents should not be cowardly. They should not back away from handling situations with their children that can be met only by intelligent and courageous action. Children should not be permitted to get away with anything. If they are permitted to do so in the home it encourages them to extend such conduct and attitude outside of the home.
>
> It is in a child's best interest to learn in his own home those things with which he will have to live for a lifetime outside of his home. The most important

thing parents can give their children is the genuine love they feel for them—the love that brought them into the world in the first place. They should not withhold that love. They should give it freely and at all times, particularly when a child is in some kind of difficulty or trouble. Parents frequently forget that some problem which appears laughably trivial to them is of major importance to a child. A child wants to be treated seriously and above all not as a child but as a person in his or her own right—as a distinctive personality—which every child is, or should be.

Both Father and Mother deplored the alarming increase in divorces. They profoundly believed in the sanctity of marriage.

"When the vow of marriage is taken," Father said many times, "it literally means, as it says, 'Until death do us part.' And it means for better or for worse.

"What sometimes brings wonderment to me is to see so many divorces come about simply because, after a few months, or a few years, they want a change—they want new partners, they want to graze in new pastures. To me this is a legalized form of promiscuity and the children are the innocent sufferers. Any human society that tolerates that kind of business eventually will find its whole moral and religious fabric worn and shoddy. I believe that the strength of ourselves as enlightened human beings centers around our ability to make our homes good, our marriages sacred, our moral and religious values enduring."

Father's only piece of advice to me as a newspaper editor came upon this subject. One day when a divorce case was before a Cleveland judge and the custody of five children was a principal issue, Father called me up.

"Louis, I think you ought to do something about this," he said. "It is a terrible thing. Here are these parents in open court dirtying up each other with their own scandalous behavior while these innocent children are being tarred with that kind of stuff for the rest of their lives. I can't understand to begin with why that judge believes it is necessary for any of these children to be in that courtroom to listen to the filth these parents are uttering about each other. There's a job for you to do, Son, and it's your business. But just as an ordinary citizen I am expressing my opinions to an editor I think ought to be doing something about it."

I don't believe there were ever two who loved each other more than Father and Mother. They were able to sit for hours in complete silence and enjoy the simple pleasure of being in each other's presence. Mother would darn and patch. Father would read or write. As the years went forward and times got better for them, their love for each other seemed to become even greater.

One day a letter came with a Hollywood postmark on it. It was an invitation to Father to come out to the movie-making capital as an adviser on an adaptation of one of his books. Anna Q. Nilsson was to be the heroine.

Mother admired Anna Q. Nilsson as an actress—on the screen. She didn't think much of the idea of Father going out to Hollywood to be on the lot where Anna Q. Nilsson was starring in a picture made from his book. She said so.

"You have no business out there, Charley," she said.

"They can make that movie without you traipsing around on one of those movie lots with all those painted-up people."

The idea momentarily intrigued Father.

"But, Ella, you could go out there with me," he said. But she wanted no part of Hollywood, either for him or for both of them.

"We stay here, Charley," she said. "I don't like those movie people. You never can tell what you're going to get into."

If the situation had been reversed Father would have felt the same way. They lived for each other.

Father didn't go to Hollywood, but Father and Mother did take many trips to the West. When he was a very young man, he had spent a little while on a ranch in New Mexico of which an uncle was part owner. Father was anxious to revisit it. He was also anxious to extend his knowledge about the West and refresh his recollection of how it looked. He and Mother began to go out to the West annually, and each time Father came back, not only with new lore about the West which he loved, but with a half dozen new ideas for novels.

From his first visit to the West in early youth, until he became successful enough to finance a return many years later, Father had depended upon diligent research and almost continuous reading for the background in his books.

He was a perfectionist. He wanted every item of descriptive matter, every article of wearing apparel, precise and indisputably correct. He studied about western horses, idioms, ranches, traditions, history, geology, towns, places. He left nothing to chance or imagination—the latter was reserved exclusively for his plot and his characters. The rest must be strictly in accord with the facts.

Thus his early books were not only creative work but also the result of meticulous and painstaking research from libraries and other reliable sources. It represented tedious and exhausting effort, but he had the necessary qualities of persistence and determination.

"It's all just as I pictured it in my mind," Father wrote back to me on his first extended trip back into the West. "I feel greatly relieved. I have always worried that I might be a little out of line now and then in some of my writing. I haven't been. I have been astonishingly correct. I feel better about that than anything else."

In his letter Father was lyrical in his praise and enthusiasm for that part of America. He found the people there real and dependable.

"Somehow living in the great spaces does something for people," he wrote. "It brings them closer to God. It brings the best that's in them out in their relationship to one another. You don't have to have anybody write up agreements out here. A man's word is all that's needed. You look into a man's eyes and you can read there all you need to know. That's the way I like it. That's why I like it out here. I only wish it were the same way all over the country."

Father and I visited together regularly. He liked to come over to our house with a new manuscript, sometimes when he had written only a few pages of it. He would sit watching me intently as I read.

"What do you think, Son, is it as good as the last one?" he would ask. He always tested out any new book on his family.

He never left an unfinished manuscript at home. When he went out driving or visiting he always took it along with him. He never worried about having anything else stolen, but he would never trust a manuscript around an unprotected house. And this included any carbon copies he made. He took all of them wherever he went.

"Just a habit," he would say. "Just a state of mind. I feel better when it's along with me. It's part of me. I wouldn't know what to do if I left it home. I'd worry about it anyway, so why shouldn't I take it with me."

As his books became more popular, and more numerous, Mother and Father made a shelf for them in his library, where they were arranged in the sequence of their publication. As each new book came out, Father would sit down, as the first thing he did, and autograph a copy for each of his children, for Mother, and as grandchildren came along, for them also. His daughters-in-law were always included.

"They're just as much my girls as our own daughters," he would say. "I hope they love me as much as I love them."

He would always lift his face for the kiss he expected when he delivered such a compliment. He always got it.

Each inscription had some quaint and affectionate

reference. He was proud of his books, but prouder of his family, and the combination of his affections showed up in the care and thought he gave to these autographs.

"Pretty attractive-looking fellow on that cover," he would say in his sly, amused way, when one of the jackets carried his picture. "No wonder all you children are so handsome."

He would always manage to say this in Mother's presence, and usually she smiled without saying anything. Father would then say, "I see the defense rests its case."

Father loved sports. He went regularly to the dingy little halls where amateur prize fights were held in Cleveland. He had never done any fighting himself, but he fancied himself as something of an expert. He always insisted that the amateur fights were more honest than the professionals.

"I like fights but I'm not good enough to tell when they're fixed," he used to say. "I know that they don't fix the amateurs, because they want to win because they have to win."

At these fights, Father made a fast friend and crony whose name was Tom Connell. Together they rarely missed a fight show. Their big black cigars contributed a substantial share to the pall of smoke that hung so heavily over the ring.

Father usually got a phone call from Tom Connell the afternoon of a fight show. Tom Connell, who was the City Fire Warden, would always say the same thing.

"Charley, I got a big job tonight at Moose Hall," he would explain. "They expect a pretty big crowd. Will you come down and help me count the house so they won't pack in more than the city fire ordinance allows in it?"

On fight nights Mother knew what was coming. Father always had some excuse.

"Ella, I guess I'll go down to the Public Library for a little while," he would carefully explain to her.

"Yes," Mother would say, "and be sure you read up on the 'Manly Art of Self Defense.' "

But she was happy when Father went to the fights, for he thoroughly enjoyed them. When he came home he was more relaxed and seemed to work more efficiently.

Father took a particular liking to one amateur, a real slugger by the name of Johnny Risko, who was short of science but long on a knockout punch. Father followed him as he fought himself out of the amateurs into the professionals. He fought everybody, including Gene Tunney, and became known as "The Spoiler" because the punishment he inflicted "softened" his opponents up for other fighters. He took quite a beating nearly every time he fought.

Father always had the same seat at the arena, next to Tom Connell, and I sat with them most of the time. Johnny always looked for Father when he fought. One night neither Tom nor Father was there and that night Johnny Risko lost. He called Father, and said, "I looked for you two fellows at the fight last night. I didn't feel right when you weren't there. Maybe that's why I lost."

I don't think Father ever again missed a Risko fight

in Cleveland, and he even went to other cities where "The Spoiler" was scheduled.

It was Risko who got Father interested in professional fights, and after he was able to afford it, Father attended the big championship fights around the country. He thought Dempsey was the greatest fighter he had ever seen and was depressed for days after Dempsey met Gene Tunney for the title on that rainy night in Philadelphia.

"Something happened there," he kept repeating over and over. "Something happened. Dempsey wasn't himself."

He went to Chicago to see the second Dempsey-Tunney fight, sure that Dempsey would win this time. The radio and the papers were full of it, and we were all eagerly awaiting Father's opinion when he came home. We were surprised when he admitted that Dempsey was "over the hill," but he added, "I am glad I have seen him in my time. There will never be another like him."

Later he followed Joe Louis for a while, but his interest in prize fighting took a noticeable drop when Dempsey got licked, and subsided after a few years. He gradually turned his attention to golf. At one time he had made fun of people who went around a big field trying to knock a poor inoffensive white ball into a lot of holes.

"That," Father would frequently say, "is my idea of about the most futile way in the world to spend your time. It looks to me just like a game for little boys who play marbles."

I don't know exactly when or under what circumstances Father changed his mind about the game of golf, but he did, and in a big way. He played it at every opportunity, on any links, with anybody. He even got Mother interested, although never more than mildly.

Father now followed the golf champions all over the country, and Mother went with him as he traveled to the tournaments where the great stars competed. He so scheduled his writing that his books were produced during the cold and gloomy winter months and spring would find him entirely free to spend his time on the golf links. When we reminded Father of his former opinion about the game, as we frequently did, he would wince in mock chagrin.

"A fellow can be wrong just a couple of times in his life, can't he?" he would say, and then quickly add, "But maybe not as wrong as I was."

Father now lived in a growing westerly suburb. He had a big rambling house with a red tile roof, and about fifteen acres of land. Back of the house he built a skeet arrangement where he would spend hours shattering the discs as an automatic device sprung them into the air. He liked for my brothers to join him, and when they were out on the skeet range their laughter came rolling back toward the house.

Father had two repressed desires. He wanted to be a successful businessman and he wanted to get into politics. The family tried to dissuade him from either venture, but he persisted.

His books were making him a great deal of money and he wanted to invest some of it. He decided to convert part of his land into a gigantic chicken hatchery and invested many thousands of dollars in the enterprise, obtaining the best equipment and superintending the job himself. But it didn't work. He was philosophical about it.

"I got taught a lesson," he said. "It was an expensive one. I won't repeat that."

But he did. He got interested in an oil-burning furnace that looked good, obtained a franchise on it for a large region, put together an organization, and set up offices. He went at it with the same enthusiasm and energy he had expended on the chicken hatchery. Like the chicken hatchery it didn't work out.

"The child went back and got his fingers burned a second time," he said, in his almost shy, modest way, a curiously charming characteristic for a man so big in physical stature, and so successful with his writing.

Father was cured of business. That left one other field of desire yet unexpressed—politics. He was tremendously interested in the little municipality in which he had built his home. He saw many things that needed to be done and he decided to run for Mayor to help accomplish them.

"Dad, why don't you do what you can as a citizen, and stick to your writing?" I asked him one day.

"Son, I got this thing in my blood, and I have to get it out," Father replied. "If I lose, all right—if I win I'll take a lick at it for a few years and see what I can do."

He was elected and he started out doing some of the things he had thought were needed. One of them was to put in a bus line. The suburb was approximately fifteen miles from downtown Cleveland, and without adequate transportation. He was determined to supply it.

The financial situation in the municipality over which he now presided as Mayor was so acute that it couldn't undertake a bus system. Father didn't let that stop him. He went to the banks and went on enough notes to finance the busses. He then went to the automobile manufacturers in Detroit and arranged to have them made and shipped. He was in business. He ran into a legal obstacle with an Ohio commission and had to spend a lot of time in Columbus getting the matter straightened out. He ran into opposition from another bus line and he moved into that. He was performing what he sincerely believed was a very important public service for the people in the community where he now made his home—and he was having a good time. It was the kind of situation that had always interested him. He always liked to fight against odds.

It was a long and rough fight, but the bus system, at last, was established.

"The easy battles of life are not even worth remembering," he said often. "It's the hard ones, the ones you don't think you've got the slightest chance of winning, and then go out and actually do win that really count."

After a few terms he gladly relinquished his job as Mayor to another. He had accomplished what he started out to do. He had put some of his own money into the bus line, but he regarded that as a neighborly investment. He was like that. He never backed away from any decision he ever made, any responsibility he ever assumed. The outcome never bothered him, provided he was sure in his own mind that he had given all he had, and had not overlooked anything that could be done.

"That's that," he would say, "and what's next on life's agenda."

There was never a son who loved or admired his father more than I did mine. He was strong in every way a man should be. He was good and clean and honorable, courageous and indomitable in his will to succeed, fair and square in his dealings with people, humble and compassionate in his attitude toward others, modest and almost retiring about himself—except about his writing, which he was proud of in a wholesome and disarming way. His devoted love for his family was reciprocated by our devoted love for him.

We all worshiped him. We all loved to be with him, to hear him talk. We were inspired by his deep, homely, logical, and yet spiritual attitude toward life and its problems.

He loved his country. He was deeply concerned about the changing world. He sensed that the United States was gradually assuming by force of circumstance a serious responsibility in the world, and he worried about whether our country was quite prepared for it.

Toward the end of his life, he thought a great deal about humanity's place in the scheme of things. He studied human history. He read extensively the findings of anthropologists, geologists, and physicists, pursuing these fields with the same will and diligence that always characterized him when anything challenged his attention.

"From almost the beginning of time," he said, "we as human beings have really been groping our way on this earth, frequently blinded by our own stupidities. We really don't know where we are going. We are trying as best we know to become civilized. We create many agencies for bringing information to ourselves.

"But there is something lacking somewhere. I don't know what it is. Maybe it's way deep inside of mankind. We are groping our way but we don't know really what that way is or where it is. Some day I would like to put these thoughts down on paper. Some day I would like to write a story about ourselves—about the gropers who inhabit this earth."

My Father wrote his last book not too long before he "went Upstairs." It was one of his best, a book he called, *So Long, Sucker*. It was, as always, a novel of the West. He brought the manuscript to my home one night and I sat down to read it. Father moved a chair over beside mine and read it with me.

"It's good, Dad," I said. "It's one of your very best."

"It better be," Father said. "It may be my last."

I looked up at him.

"Why do you say that, Dad?" I asked him.

"A fellow has to stop writing some time, doesn't he?" Father said.

I thought then that he meant he was preparing to put

the cover over his typewriter, and call it a literary career.

But that wasn't it. He became ill. Father had always abhorred hospitals. He associated them with members of his family who had been taken there and didn't come back. He wanted to stay in his own home. Mother watched over him day and night, sensing that there was something really and seriously wrong. Finally the doctor warned us that he would have to be moved to a hospital in order to pull through.

As the oldest in the family I was chosen to talk with Father, to reason out the hospital question with him. It was a hard thing to attempt, but I sat down beside his bed and talked with him. He listened. At last he said:

"Son, I always wanted you boys in particular to decide things for yourselves, to make decisions. Apparently you've made one now for me. I don't want to leave my home, but if you believe I should go to a hospital I'll go."

We got him ready for the hospital. His condition was critical, and by this time he sensed it. He looked at each one of us and he smiled, as the men were about to wheel him to the ambulance.

In a soft voice, and with a small wave of his hand, he quoted the title from the last book he wrote:

"So Long, Sucker!"

He did not come back home.

He was a great man—a very great man—and for the son who writes these words now, the greatest man it was ever my privilege to know.

Mother lived fifteen years after Father went away. Not long ago I sat once more before a typewriter with my tears blurring the keys. I sat for a long while thinking about Mother as I had sat thinking about Father. At last I wrote the following paragraphs about Mother, and I include them here as they appeared in The Cleveland Press the day after she was called away to join Father:

There were the days, when we were very small children, when she washed, scrubbed, ironed, mended clothes, cooked, sat up all night with us when we were sick, never seemed to stop working.

She was up long before anyone else in the dark of morning. She was the last to fall asleep long after everyone else had gone to bed.

There were the days, too, when she lifted the flagging spirits of our father, discouraged by the steady flow of rejection slips for stories he sent to publishers.

Our home at Fulton and Seymour centered around her, was built around her courage, her belief in her family, her determination that they succeed in what they undertook to do.

She was not concerned about the world outside of her own home. She liked her neighbors. She did many considerate things for them. But the great, vast world outside took secondary place. Her home, and those in it, were her responsibility above all else.

Her love, respect and fierce devotion to her husband were legend throughout the neighborhood. Her insistence that her children be good, clean and well-behaved was equally recognized and respected. She required that her children see their responsibility and accept it. She made them, in her own oft-repeated words, "toe the mark."

"As the twig is bent so grows the tree," she quoted so often that it became something of a family by-word.

299

She saw her husband, a carpenter by trade, become a successful novelist, and read in manuscript form practically everything he had ever written. She saw him first write under a kerosene lamp with a scratchy pen on borrowed brown wrapping paper in the kitchen and with his success move into his own study, which she furnished and watched over as the sacred place in her home.

Into the hearts and minds of her children she put her own strong religious principles and emphasized repeatedly the elementary distinctions between right and wrong.

Her husband went to his eternal sleep 15 years ago after a brief illness. She lived the years since his death in her own apartment, on the second floor of the family's house at 1345 West Blvd., as she wished, surrounded by the books her husband had written, by his pictures, by the pictures and reminders of her children, her grandchildren, her great-grandchildren.

Last evening, near midnight, she followed her husband into eternal sleep in a room at Fairview Park Hospital.

My mother was a devoted, tireless, courageous woman, whose greatest love was reserved for her husband and her children. She is with my father now and we all know that there, with him, she is happy.

Chapter 28

TED COOPER is a nice young fellow. I like him. I hope he likes me. I have known him for something like thirteen years. He is now almost exactly the age at which I left public school to take my first job forty-five years ago.

I met Ted Cooper a few hours after he was born. He is one of our five grandchildren.

I am just like any other grandparent—I am greatly interested in our grandchildren: Leigh, aged fifteen, whom I know as "The Princess"; her small and lively sister, Laura, aged four; and our son's two handsome sons, Charles, aged four, and Robert, two, who live in far-off Las Cruces, New Mexico.

My first interest in them is the natural one of all grandparents. There is another interest. It is the interest in the kind of world in which they are likely to live.

Ted and I take walks. We talk. As we hike along, my mind persists in these thoughts:

Here we are, two human beings, tied together by blood, but separated by two complete generations—and living, for practical purposes, in totally different worlds.

His is a world I did not dream of when I was his age. It didn't then exist. The world in which he now lives is for him rather commonplace, and he eagerly looks forward to a still different and more amazing world.

He thinks and talks of things it is hard for me to imagine. He knows they will happen. He takes the happening of them for granted.

I wish it were possible for me to trade places with him. He will live—together with his sisters and cousins and all others of their age, not alone in America but throughout the earth—in the most wonderful and exciting world that human beings have ever experienced from the time they first walked upright on this curious planet spinning in infinite space.

I am an incorrigible optimist. History, as I see it, supports that attitude. Certainly human history tends to liquidate the pessimist.

I believe that human beings are constantly getting better. I also believe that the circumstances of life in one generation prepare youth for the one which is to follow. The hot-rodder of today is tomorrow's jet pilot.

The increased tempo of life in these times is simply a conditioning process for what inevitably lies ahead. The earlier maturing of our sons and daughters is Nature's way of attuning them to a vastly different world which is as yet undefined, but which is just as certain as tomorrow's coming. The children of these days are an advance over their parents, as our own children were over us. It is Nature's law.

If only I had another twenty-five—or fifty—years to see for myself this fabulous new world! Since I am reasonably sure this will be denied me, I should like to set down here my own notions of what it may be like for my grandchildren, and their generation—this brand-new world of 1980, and thereafter.

It will be, first of all, as might be expected, a world of many more people, for man is multiplying in incredible numbers.

Two-and-a-half billion on the earth now. In two decades, another billion.

In the United States now 165 million. By 2000 A.D., 300 million.

The world shrinks.

Man springs a projectile 300 miles into the air and straightens it out at 18,000 miles an hour around the earth. He puts space platforms above the land and holds them there by natural forces which he learns to manipulate.

He puts the atom to peaceful use, draws power from the sun to run his electrical appliances, draws power into his home by the shingles with which he roofs his house.

He controls weather. He makes rain to fall and sun to shine at will. He takes salt from the oceans covering two-thirds of the global land mass. He makes the desert bloom. He makes a garden of the barren places on the earth.

Malthus said man would reproduce faster than the land would sustain him. It didn't happen. It won't. Surplus already confounds the scarcity Malthus feared, and already complicates our national politics. Malthus overlooked a few facts: man's ingenuity, man's insatiable curiosity about his world, his indomitable purpose to make it work for him.

What, therefore, of this future for today's grandchildren? Is it good? Is it bad? Is it foreboding, Is it hopeful?

We are a strange people, we earthbound creatures with sky-bound impulses. We—particularly in America.

We reflect our times. We are a part of them, for the nature of the times at any given moment exerts an irrevocable influence upon our outlook.

If times are bad, we think they will be forever bad.

If times are good, we think they will be forever good.

Neither happens.

We move irresistibly forward—a setback here, a mighty surge forward there.

We, young, dynamic, restless, eager, flexible, explosive, are the wonder of our times.

Nothing like us has ever before happened.

We are the unique product of freedom, incentive, opportunity, ceaseless ferment, interminable self-searching, continuous soul examination and prodding conscience—unending revolution by ballot.

We always will be.

In my own lifetime I have seen three generations of

America—three ways of life so different that they might almost be described as distinct "civilizations."

I overheard my grandfather, Lucien Bonaparte Seltzer, say to my father in 1907, when I was ten:

"Son, the United States is through, washed up. It will never be the same. It's done for."

My grandfather was right when he thought that the country would never again be the same. But it was not "washed up" or "done for."

My grandfather had lived in a country where wood was cut for the fire; where food was either slaughtered on the farm, or bought by bulk from a store reached by wagon over miles of corrugated dirt roads; where stereopticon was incredible; where life was both leisurely and communal, tempo slow, problems relatively few, life largely sustained by beneficence of the elements.

At the very time my grandfather was making his prophecy of national doom, the scientists, the industrialists, the physicists were combining their talents to push benefits at the American people in greater profusion and in a shorter time than ever before; and these benefits were to alter life more completely and abruptly than at any other time in human history.

Images were to move across screens. Machines were to fly in the air. Ships were to travel under water. Autos were to thread their way over thousands of miles of highways. Voices and music were to be sent thousands of miles without wires. Thermostats were to order the exact degree of heat for human comfort. Water was to come forth crystal-clear by the simple turn of a faucet.

A thousand other things, now too commonplace to enumerate, were literally catapulted at us from laboratory and assembly line.

Life in the United States of America, as Grandpa Lucien asserted, was, indeed, never to be the same again.

In 1939 my own father, Charles Alden Seltzer, who had scoffed at my grandfather's prophecy of doom in 1907, said to me in the living room of my home:

"Son, the United States of America is through, washed up. It will never be the same. It's done for."

My grandfather, in 1907, made his prophecy as one distinctive way of life in these United States had ended, and another, a vastly greater one, was beginning.

My father, in 1939, made his prophecy likewise, when a distinctive way of life was ending and another, a vastly greater one, was about to begin.

We now embark upon the third, and perhaps the most remarkable, of our "civilizations." Surely more will follow.

Today, despite the confusion, bewilderment, uncertainty, internal social, economic, and political divisions, the atmosphere of inconsistency and conflict, the despair, the disjointed outlook of the country and the world itself—today, the United States is entering, without our especially realizing it, upon a newer, a vastly greater age.

This age of electronics, of radar, of television, of atomic power, of solar energy, of things now only in scientific and technological swaddling clothes, will exert even greater change upon the whole of life than any which preceded it.

It will carry us—as certainly and immutably as the forward thrust of life itself, as the rising and setting of tomorrow's sun—to greater prosperity, greater human happiness and equity, and, I believe, to greater economic and social stability.

This third "civilization" will be as completely revolutionary in its ultimate effects, as the automobile—airplane—radio—television—movie civilization was, in contrast with the horse and wagon—stereopticon—coal bucket–kerosene lamp–water well civilization of my own boyhood.

We will see changes far greater in scope and effect during the next twenty-five years than any seen in the past fifty.

We know that a single secret of the celestial outer spaces, disclosed to the inquiring mind and eye of the scientist, opens vistas to many other secrets in a fabulously multiplying fashion. Equally is this true of the industrial technologist who translates the findings of the scientist into the realities of everyday life.

We live at a constantly accelerated pace. We cannot stop it. We cannot declare a moratorium—a sabbatical—to the forward march of science and technology. It is not in man's nature to do so.

My grandfather and my father were the finest and most sincere men I have ever known, among the most discerning and alert, but they were deceived by the apparently irrevocable nature of their times. Perhaps, this was because change in their time was less frequent, and more perceptible. When it came it seemed sharp and abrupt, revolutionary and upsetting.

This is no longer true. We are caught up in the swift and tumultuous whirlpools of incredibly unfolding change. We expect it. We take it for granted. Each new thing brings only momentary arching of eyebrows. We adapt ourselves quickly.

So now we face a brand-new age, the greatest of all. Out of it will emerge the greatest United States of America in all our dynamic history. And yet most of us, accustomed as we are to change, scarcely notice.

There will be physical changes which defy the imagination, and paralleling them, the greatest advance mankind has ever witnessed in social, spiritual, and cultural areas. Inevitably we will elevate and strengthen the underfed, the underclothed, the undersheltered, the undereducated, the overdominated peoples of the earth—those whose number we loosely approximate at two-thirds of all who draw breath each day.

What all of this will do to man's spirit is a separate question—and a basic challenge to humanity.

Man's ego tends to rise with his own accomplishments. In the days when he was required to fell the tree in the forest for shelter, rely upon kindly elements for food, track down animals for clothing, he felt insignificant, impotent, apprehensive, against the vastnesses of land, sky and air with which he was surrounded.

As he put up skyscrapers, made machines work for him, sent vehicles through the air, automobiles over land, ships under water, made images to move on screens, sent rockets and missiles at remote targets with uncanny precision, exploded bombs, conquered disease, prolonged life—in proportion to these accomplishments his ego expanded and his faith in something Big and Providential apart from himself shrank.

In moments of preoccupation with material accomplishments, man has always experienced misgivings— and we in our time have not been immune to them.

For a long time we, as Americans, have experienced singular bodily comforts—and paradoxically, sore anguish of heart and spirit. Strange inexplicable yearnings persist. By trial, by error, by torment, we are tardily realizing that there is something more important than physical accomplishment even when achieved in such astonishing pattern and significance as during the last half century.

We now search more deeply, more questioningly, more anxiously, as we pass the midpoint of the epochal twentieth century.

As we comprehend the spiritual vacuum created by diverting ourselves so exclusively to the flow of material benefits, we now wisely seek for balance—to accomplish what was denied other great civilizations which flowered and withered and were blown away. We have gained wisdom in America—the wisdom of a child who eats too much candy, who puts fingers to fire.

And in this new wisdom we are spiritually and morally restrengthening ourselves for the greatest experience this nation has ever enjoyed.

What, therefore, of this future for today's grandchildren?

I wish it were possible to trade places with them.

It will be great and wondrous. It will, I profoundly believe, come very close to the peace on earth and good will among men—for all colors and kinds—which mankind, deep in its collective heart, has always hoped for. There is, after all, one man under God, in one world. Science is steadily shrinking it to that one world. It simply cannot be stopped.

Everywhere mankind is making a mighty effort to throw off the restricting shackles of prejudice, discrimination, illiteracy, backwardness, domination by others. Man wants to be free, in both mind and spirit. And, wanting it, he will be free.

The scientific accomplishments of our century dwarf anything man has seen in the past, and the spiritual accomplishments of the future will dwarf anything thus far achieved.

And now—

Could I—or anyone else—do again at the early age I began what has been recounted in this book?

Ed Murrow asked me this question one evening when he brought his "Person to Person" show into our home.

I said no. The law wouldn't allow it for one thing. A boy of thirteen cannot work at a regular job today.

Along with all other professions and businesses, ours is now highly specialized and complicated. Even if the law today were to permit an uneducated thirteen-year-old boy to go into our business, he would be utterly lost. He might somehow, if a genius, come through, but I doubt it. Conditions have changed unbelievably. It is now almost imperative that we have adequately educated reporters and executives.

Our grandchildren are often told that it was an advantage to be born when their grandparents were, but their world of tomorrow will more than offset any advantages of the past.

The thirteen-year-old boy of today will do things I never dreamed of.

Thus, I end my first book, saying as I do so—

In God, I believe. My Country, I love. For its future I have, as you will observe, profound and abiding faith.

And to all who have made my life, up to the very moment I write these words, possible and endurable and pleasant—and, I hope, useful—I am eternally indebted. And I am indebted, likewise, to those in my family, my paper, my home town, who persist in making me look better than I know in my heart I am.

I have looked back—I have looked at today—I have looked at tomorrow.

The years have been both hard and good, but when the totting-up is finished—THE YEARS WERE GOOD.

INDEX

313

LOUIS BENSON SELTZER was born September 19, 1897, in a single-story cottage back of a fire station on Cleveland's near West Side—on the other side of the river and the other side of the tracks. The oldest of five children in a household always short of cash, he was hardly in knee britches before he was handling a paper route to help out the kitchen bank. His father was Charles Alden Seltzer, who was to write 49 books, many of which were later made into motion pictures. But when Louis Seltzer was seven years old his father had not yet sold his first story, and when he was thirteen he left school without finishing seventh grade in order to take a job as an office boy and cub reporter on *The Leader.* A year later he moved over to *The Cleveland News,* only to come back to *The Leader* where, in addition to his other duties, he wrote a column under the by-line of "Luee, The Offis Boy." Once more he shifted to *The Cleveland*

News, and after a short time there he was fired—
and told he'd never make a newspaperman.

Louis Seltzer then spent a little over a year writing copy for an advertising agency—a job he hated,
for he was determined to be a newspaperman.
Quitting his job in disgust he talked himself into
another job—on *The Cleveland Press,* where he
has been ever since.

This was early in 1915 and Louis B. Seltzer was
not quite eighteen. He was already married to
Marion Elizabeth Champlin, and his first child,
Chester Ellsworth, was soon to be born. A daughter, Shirley Marion, was born in 1919. Within a
year of joining *The Press* he was made City Editor, only to fire himself from that particular assignment in six months because he didn't like the
desk work. He chose to become a reporter again,
specializing in the political beat.

In 1921 he again became City Editor of *The
Press.* In 1924 he was named Political Editor. In
1927 he was made Chief Editorial Writer. In
March of 1928 he became Associate Editor. And
on July 9, in the same year, he was elevated to the
post of Editor of *The Cleveland Press,* a position
he has filled ever since. In addition he has been
since 1937 Editor-in-Chief of the Scripps-Howard
Newspapers of Ohio.

(continued from front flap)

aster relief, and has actively helped "make" some of Ohio's most distinguished public officeholders. He has himself turned down an appointment to the United States Senate, and innumerable offers of bigger jobs in bigger cities. For to him the fact that he is affectionately known to tens of thousands of men and women as "Mr. Cleveland" is the most important fact in his life. When you have finished reading the warm and personal story of this newspaperman's newspaperman you will find yourself wishing that there could be men like Louis B. Seltzer on every newspaper in the country—men so dedicated to their town and their work that they have become symbols in their own lifetime.

BRUCE CATTON, in his Intro-duction, says: "You don't always know, at the moment, when you are brushing elbows with somebody special. I first saw Louis B. Seltzer one summer day, thirty-five years ago or thereabouts, when as a very junior reporter I was covering the Cuyahoga County Court House for The Cleveland News. . . . it was quite a few years before I realized that I had then met one of the most remarkable men whom the rather unusual city of Cleveland has produced in this century. . . . This career has had an impact which has often driven strong men to the use of very strong language, but its ultimate effect has been very good indeed. It would be possible to argue that he is today the best and most effective news-paper editor in America."

Jacket design by H. Lawrence Hoffman